First World War
and Army of Occupation
War Diary
France, Belgium and Germany

27 DIVISION
Headquarters, Branches and Services
Royal Army Medical Corps
Assistant Director Medical Services
19 December 1914 - 31 December 1915

WO95/2256/2

The Naval & Military Press Ltd
www.nmarchive.com
Published in association with The National Archives

Published by

The Naval & Military Press Ltd

Unit 10 Ridgewood Industrial Park,

Uckfield, East Sussex,

TN22 5QE England

Tel: +44 (0) 1825 749494

www.naval-military-press.com

www.nmarchive.com

This diary has been reprinted in facsimile from the original. Any imperfections are inevitably reproduced and the quality may fall short of modern type and cartographic standards.

© Crown Copyright
Images reproduced by permission of The National Archives, London, England, 2015.

Contents

Document type	Place/Title	Date From	Date To
Heading	WO95/2256/2		
Heading	27th Division Medical Asst Director Medical Services Dec 1914-Dec 1915		
Miscellaneous	ADMS. 27th Division Vol I Dec 1914 Jan 1915		
War Diary	Winchester	19/12/1914	21/12/1914
War Diary	Havre	22/12/1914	23/12/1914
War Diary	Arques	25/12/1914	04/01/1915
War Diary	Borre	05/01/1915	05/01/1915
War Diary	Boeschepe	06/01/1915	31/01/1915
Miscellaneous	Inoculation Return 27th Division.		
Heading	A.D.M.S. 27th Division Vol II Feb 1915		
Miscellaneous	A.D.M.S. 27th Div Feb 1915		
War Diary	Boeschepe	01/02/1915	04/02/1915
War Diary	Reninghelst	05/02/1915	28/02/1915
Heading	ADMS. 27th Division Vol III March 1915		
War Diary	Reninghelst	01/03/1915	31/03/1915
Heading	A.D.M.S. 27th Division Vol IV April 1915		
War Diary	Reninghelst	01/04/1915	04/04/1915
War Diary	Reninghelst Ypres	05/04/1915	05/04/1915
War Diary	Ypres	06/04/1915	23/04/1915
War Diary	Poperinghe	24/04/1915	26/04/1915
War Diary	L'ebbe Poperinghe	27/04/1915	27/04/1915
War Diary	L'ebbe Farm	28/04/1915	29/04/1915
War Diary	Lebbe Farm Poperinghe	30/04/1915	30/04/1915
Miscellaneous	Extract From D.O.3rd April 1915		
Miscellaneous	Extract From D.O.8th April 1915		
Miscellaneous	Medical Officer i/c Regt	03/04/1915	03/04/1915
Heading	ADMS 27th Division Vol V May 1915		
War Diary	Ebbe-Farm Poperinghe	01/05/1915	02/05/1915
War Diary	Ebbe-Farm	03/05/1915	15/05/1915
War Diary	Ebbe-Farm Poperinghe	16/05/1915	16/05/1915
War Diary	Ebbe-Farm	17/05/1915	18/05/1915
War Diary	Ebbe-Farm Poperinghe	19/05/1915	24/05/1915
War Diary	Ebbe-Farm	24/05/1915	30/05/1915
War Diary	Ebbe-Farm Poperinghe	31/05/1915	31/05/1915
Miscellaneous	Acting A.D.M.S., 27th Division.	28/05/1915	28/05/1915
Heading	27th Division ADMS 27th Division Vol VI June 1915		
War Diary	Croix Du Bac	01/06/1915	30/06/1915
Miscellaneous	Divisional Routine Orders No. 4 By Major General T. D'O. Snow, C.B. Commanding 27th. Division.	02/06/1915	02/06/1915
Miscellaneous	Divisional Routine Orders-No.13 By Major General T. D'O. Snow, C.B., Commanding 27th. Division.	13/06/1915	13/06/1915
Heading	Divisional Routine Orders. No.14 By Major General T. D'O. Snow, C.B., Commanding 27th. Division.	14/06/1915	14/06/1915
Miscellaneous	Divisional Routine Orders No.15 By Major General T. D'O. Snow, C.B., Commanding 27th. Division.	15/06/1915	15/06/1915
Miscellaneous	Divisional Routine Orders No.22 By Major General T. D'O. Snow, U.B., Commanding 27th Division	22/06/1915	22/06/1915
Miscellaneous	Divisional Routine Orders, No.23 By Major General T. D'O. Snow, C.B., Commanding 27th. Division.	23/06/1915	23/06/1915

Miscellaneous	President. Lieut. Colonel A.R. Liddell, A.S.C., Commanding 27th Divisional Train		
Miscellaneous	Divisional Routine Orders No. 24 By Major General T. D'O. Snow, C.E., Commanding 27th Division.	24/06/1915	24/06/1915
Heading	27th Division A.D.M.S. 27th Division Vol VII From 1st To 31st July 1915		
Miscellaneous	A.D.M.S. 27th Div. July 1915		
War Diary	Croix Du Bac	01/07/1915	31/07/1915
Miscellaneous	Divisional Routine Orders, No. 32 By Major General T.D. Snow, K.C.B. Commanding 27th Division.	02/07/1915	02/07/1915
Miscellaneous	Divisional Routine Orders, No. 36 By Major General T. D'O. Snow, K.C.B., Commanding 27th. Division.	06/07/1915	06/07/1915
Operation(al) Order(s)	Divisional Routine Orders, No. 48 by Major General G.F. Milne, C.B.,D.S.O., Commanding 27th. Division	19/07/1915	19/07/1915
Operation(al) Order(s)	Divisional Routine Orders, No. 48 by Major General G.F. Milne, C.B.,D.S.O., Commanding 27th. Division	30/07/1915	30/07/1915
Heading	27th Division ADMS 27th Division Vol VIII Aug Vol 15		
Miscellaneous	A.D.M.S. 27th Div Aug 1915		
War Diary	Croix Du Bac	01/08/1915	31/08/1915
Miscellaneous	Divisional Order No. 388th Of 2nd August, 1915		
Operation(al) Order(s)	Divisional Routine Orders, No.66 by Major General G.F. Milne, C.B.,D.S.O., Commanding 27th. Division	06/08/1915	06/08/1915
Operation(al) Order(s)	Divisional Routine Orders, No.66 by Major General G.F. Milne, C.B.,D.S.O., Commanding 27th. Division	11/08/1915	11/08/1915
Operation(al) Order(s)	Divisional Routine Orders, No.66 by Major General G.F. Milne, C.B.,D.S.O., Commanding 27th. Division	18/08/1915	18/08/1915
Operation(al) Order(s)	Divisional Routine Orders, No.66 by Major General G.F. Milne, C.B.,D.S.O., Commanding 27th. Division	23/08/1915	23/08/1915
Operation(al) Order(s)	Divisional Routine Orders, No.66 by Major General G.F. Milne, C.B.,D.S.O., Commanding 27th. Division	31/08/1915	31/08/1915
Miscellaneous			
Heading	27th Division A.D.M.S. 27th Division Vol IX Sept 15		
Miscellaneous	May Have Been Detached		
War Diary	Croix Du Bac	01/09/1915	15/09/1915
War Diary	Merris	16/09/1915	18/09/1915
War Diary	Warfusee Abancourt	18/09/1915	19/09/1915
War Diary	Warfusee	20/09/1915	20/09/1915
War Diary	Mericourt	21/09/1915	30/09/1915
Miscellaneous	Monthly Inoculation Return		
Operation(al) Order(s)	Divisional Routine Orders, No. 110. by Major General G.F. Milne, C.B., D.S.O., Commanding 27th Division.	23/09/1915	23/09/1915
Operation(al) Order(s)	Divisional Routine Orders, No. 110. by Major General G.F. Milne, C.B., D.S.O., Commanding 27th Division.	24/09/1915	24/09/1915
Operation(al) Order(s)	Divisional Routine Orders, No. 110. by Major General G.F. Milne, C.B., D.S.O., Commanding 27th Division.	25/09/1915	25/09/1915
Miscellaneous	Map Reference 27th Divn And Posts Etc Sheet 36 1/20,000		
Heading	A.D.M.S 27th Dn Oct 15 Vol X		
War Diary	Mericourt	01/10/1915	26/10/1915
War Diary	Bovelles	27/10/1915	30/10/1915
Operation(al) Order(s)	Divisional Routine Orders, No. 117 by Major General G.F. Milne, C.B.,D.S.O., Commanding 27th Division	01/10/1915	01/10/1915
Miscellaneous	Divisional Routine Orders, No. 117 by Major General G.F. Milne, C.B.,D.S.O., Commanding 27th Division	04/10/1915	04/10/1915

Operation(al) Order(s)	Divisional Routine Orders, No. 117 by Major General G.F. Milne, C.B.,D.S.O., Commanding 27th Division	05/10/1915	05/10/1915
Operation(al) Order(s)	Divisional Routine Orders, No. 117 by Major General G.F. Milne, C.B.,D.S.O., Commanding 27th Division	14/10/1915	14/10/1915
Miscellaneous	Monthly Inoculation Return		
Heading	A.D.M.S. 27th Div Nov Vol XI Nov 1915		
War Diary	Bovelles	01/11/1915	30/11/1915
Heading	ADMS 27 Div Dec Vol XII		
War Diary	Bovelles France	01/12/1915	31/12/1915

WO 95/2256/2

27TH DIVISION
MEDICAL

ASST DIRECTOR MEDICAL SERVICES

DEC 1914 - DEC 1915

A.D.M.S. 27th Division.

Vol I.

Oct "14
Dec '15

12/4/1914
June 1915
5 Jan 1915

Army Form C. 2118.

WAR DIARY
or
INTELLIGENCE SUMMARY.
(Erase heading not required.)

Instructions regarding War Diaries and Intelligence Summaries are contained in F.S. Regs., Part II. and the Staff Manual respectively. Title pages will be prepared in manuscript.

Hour, Date, Place	Summary of Events and Information	Remarks and references to Appendices
19th Dec. 1914 Winchester	1st & 81st Infantry Brigades and 20th & 27th Field Ambulances embarked at Southampton for Havre undertaken by 14th squadron of Transport. Went to Havre, and two Ambulance wagons to pick up party – 10 picked up – 5 of whom guard of war ships same night.	
20th Dec. 1914 Winchester	1st Brigade R.H.A. and 80th Infantry Brigade left – one officer (Lieut A. Rendell of 83rd F.A.) and two Ambulance wagons as pick up party – no men kept back.	
21st Dec. 1914 Winchester	Headquarters R.E., A.S.C. Train R.A.B. and 81st, 82nd, 83rd Field Ambulances left by march route to Southampton and left for Havre about 8.30 pm in 4 ships.	
22nd Dec. 1914 Havre	Arrived Havre, Headquarter ships about 11 am. She entrained at once & units remained under cover at "Pondichéry" for the night & subsequently went into No 3 Camp.	
23rd Dec. 1914 Havre 24th Dec 1914 Bergues	Headquarters entrained at Havre du Marchandise 5 bn left about 6.30 pm for Rouen. Train arrived at Bergues at 1.30 pm – Full Ambulances not arrived and expected shortly, tomorrow. 82nd and 83rd F.A. reporting arrived and asking instructions to disposal given. Officer of A.D.M.S. Establishes at VEERMERSH. Two 3rd Ambulances at BERGUES. 81st F.A. at HIRR-givin, 80th F.A. at BERLINGHEM. R.Y.A. Brigade at RENESOUR, SERCUS and BOESEGHEM. Three Motor Ambulances sent by 82nd F.A. – Reported for temporary duty with the 5th Division.	

J. M. Macpherson
J. Macpherson

WAR DIARY
or
INTELLIGENCE SUMMARY.
(Erase heading not required.)

Army Form C. 2118.

Hour, Date, Place	Summary of Events and Information	Remarks and references to Appendices
25 Dec 1914 ARQUES	A.D.M.S. visited AIRE area — D.A.D.M.S. Blaringhem area morning & for dispersal March 8 to 10.10. Staff Captain all ready & A Field Q.M.S. who arrived at Arques 6.30 p.m. the latter detrained and proceeded to billets & the former went by train to Aire. Second half of 83rd Field Amb and the 82nd Field Ambulance arrived Arques at 6.30 pm detrained and proceeded to Billets 83rd at ARQUES and 82nd to BLARINGHEM. Two Ambulance wagons of 82nd Fld Amb left behind owing to breakdown of Railway wagon.	
26th Dec 1914 ARQUES	Field Ambulances established Collecting Stations in their respective Brigade Areas, one car of Typhoid reported from 82nd Brigade, he was left behind in Divisional Hospital Havre, whence he was reported as short, was called for from 82nd Brigade. A.D.M.S. visited 82nd Brigade area BLARINGHEM.	
27th Dec 1914 ARQUES	Took over of sick & Arrangements completed by M.O. ¼ B.L. Brigade R.F.A. S.M.O. 82nd Brigade informed where to place area out of bounds. Twenty one Motor Ambulances arrived ARQUES A.D.M.S. visited AIRE, inspected transport of 81st Field Amb. and arranged re transfer of sick.	
28 Dec 1914 ARQUES	Motor ambulance cars distributed as follows; 9 to 81st F/A, 6 to 82nd F/Amb., 6 to 83rd F/Amb., the workshop lorry to 81st F/A Amb. The three Motor Ambulances belonging to A.D.M.S. returned to No 1 M.A.C. A further requisition was published on Divisional orders regarding construction of French Latrines & keep existing arrangements in which the feeding of men depends.	

J Maitland
Major

WAR DIARY
or
INTELLIGENCE SUMMARY
(Erase heading not required.)

Army Form C. 2118.

Hour, Date, Place	Summary of Events and Information	Remarks and references to Appendices
29 Dec 1914 ARQUES	Sudden increase of Typhoid incidence had commenced. Inspection of Brigades & Batteries as matter of special urgency. A.D.M.S. visited D.F.W.S., Y.G., F.A., B.m.	
30th Dec 1914 ARQUES	All units commenced Typhoid inoculation to complete. Anywhere inoculations ad nauseam to be. to protest having to be daily. A.D.M.S visited Dunkerque. Arrangements for inoculation reference bodies between the Cavalier Brigade. D.A.D.M.S. visited Bethune to consult H.A.M.C. 1st Division in reference to general medical management.	
31st Dec 1914 ARQUES	A.D.M.S inspected transport section 83 & 84 field Amb. Total sick admitted to date to Divisional Hospitals from 29.11. Oct '14 79. Temperance Div. at ARQUES is 330 — for influenza & frost bite. Total sick admitted. Diphtheria to date. Previous Total number of inoculations Friday 3rd S. No. of Sick Evacuations.	M.P. Yeatman Lieut Col R.A.M.C.

WAR DIARY
or
INTELLIGENCE SUMMARY.
(Erase heading not required.)

Army Form C. 2118.

Instructions regarding War Diaries and Intelligence Summaries are contained in F.S. Regs., Part II. and the Staff Manual respectively. Title pages will be prepared in manuscript.

Hour, Date, Place	Summary of Events and Information	Remarks and references to Appendices
JAN. 1st Aug 15 ARQUES	Reported unsanitary conditions prevailing at ARQUES especially in vicinity of the Regimental Manure — etc. — MO. also visits intend accordingly.	
2.5 " "	B.M. & Army visited board and gave advice of the various points of medical arrangement at ARQUES. Instructions to cease from this date to anticipate hospitalisation beyond civilian care from all ranks will never exceed 85%. Estab. Square cases inspected by MOs who examined rare entirely unavailable as regards Linen and Body	See Return hereunder attached
3.5 " "	Strong Advisory Council convened and to hospital especially as relates to proposed visits Sanitary Inspection of training Equipment Sanitary Field Hospital R.O. was made advisable to dispense of slight cases of sick to be employed near H.Q.M.S. in others than trenches variant to undergo convalescence — these cases made to march & diet and A.T.O. Stationary Hospital. R.A. we visited to-day. O.K.O aide attempts to incarceration of slight cases of sickness unable to march, accumulated at R.A.P. about 50 cases admits to Nos. Stationary Hospitals	
4th " "	Otherwise no marked change to Remarks	
5th " BORRE	Part of Head Qrs. including Medical Personnel left Argues on route to the front arrived the night at BORRE, F.A.O with Ambulance left Blaringhem to the Front and arrived to-day at HAZEBROUCK No. 3h Ambulance Road	
6th " BOESCHEPE	Ad. Qrs. to BORRE. A.S.M.S moved ahead at BAILLEUL also Advance Dept of Medical Stores and Clearing Hospital at BAILLEUL ST. JANS CHAPPEL and forming Station of Nos. 46 Amb.	J Munro[?]

Army Form C. 2118.

WAR DIARY
or
INTELLIGENCE SUMMARY.
(Erase heading not required.)

Instructions regarding War Diaries and Intelligence Summaries are contained in F.S. Regs., Part II. and the Staff Manual respectively. Title pages will be prepared in manuscript.

Hour, Date, Place	Summary of Events and Information	Remarks and references to Appendices
10th Jan. 1915 BOESCHEPE	R.A.M.C. operation orders in duplication issued, arrangements of sick and wounded evacuation – Shortly stated as follows: – Field Ambulance No I attached to Brigade in firing line in readiness for picking post and Advanced Dressing Station. Field Ambulance No II with supporting Brigade will deal with casual sick of the Brigade and even No I with minor of the army and also from and wounded. Brigade washing and disinfesting Post. Field Ambulance No III with Resting Brigade will treat casual sick of its own Brigade, also farm and maintain a Divisional convalescent depôt. Each Field Ambulance to collection of Sick. Two Ambulances to evacuate its own sick with its own Ambulances. No I to apply to No II and No III if necessary. Two convoys to be sent each day, 10 A.M. and 2 P.M. Motors of No I Fd. Amb. not to be used for afternoon convoy. Each Fd. Ambulance to detail a Sanitary Officer for its Brigade Area. Provision laundries in Locrehoeck, also improving the means of purification of water supply in this Area.	II

WAR DIARY
or
INTELLIGENCE SUMMARY.
(Erase heading not required.)

Army Form C. 2118.

Hour, Date, Place	Summary of Events and Information	Remarks and references to Appendices
6th JAN. 1915. BOSSCHEPE	Part of Head qrs and Medical Personnel arrived BOSSCHEPE. Rest yet to arrive with Staff. Bde HqR AIRE en route for the front. B.3.5. Fld Amb. arrived DICKEBUSCH late at night.	J Mahon MajorGenl
7th	4 Offrs and 85 men evacuated sick from Bde Hd Qrs and returned to unit. Building rented in area of RENNINGHELST also selected building for Rennoy Clothes for 630 pairs Ambulances in DICKEBUSCH and suggested vicinity of collecting Post. Immatulum arranged & Medical Work and Regimental Medical Officers on subject of field arrangements evacuation of sick and wounded. Handed in with General Stafford important work. Officers left at ST OMER. Pro Pet Amt. arrived near OUDENDON late at night unable to reach billets.	
8th	4th Fd. Bde. 1 Officer and 18 other Ranks Wounded. Other Ranks at all concerned & BAILLEUL. Notified needed DICKEBUSCH B.3.5 and First Fld Ambulance First Fd. Amb. arrived BOSSCHEPE and took billets in farms one mile distant. Received orders re formation of Brigade sanitary sections (Coms B) sundry sanitary Offrs. New formations. Received & Sanitary details. 1 Officer and 25 other Ranks received (specials) by Coml 4b. BAILLEUL ready to join Division. Re Medical disposition at present known are, asking all rounds from Liverton. 1- Collecting Post near WIERSTAAT. Receiving Station near DICKEBUSCH and evacuating by cars Motor Amb. to BAILLEUL and 3 Clearing hospital.	J Mahon MajorGenl

111

WAR DIARY
or
INTELLIGENCE SUMMARY.
(Erase heading not required.)

Army Form C. 2118.

Hour, Date, Place	Summary of Events and Information	Remarks and references to Appendices
9th Jan 1914 BOESCHEPE.	Sick Officers 1 Other Ranks 48 WOUNDED Officers 2 Other Ranks 37. Arrangements commenced for moving a Brigade Bath and Wash houses in Brewery at Boeschepe to be formed and maintained by No III Field Amb. Great difficulty in obtaining suitable accommodation for all troops. Situation obviated and taken over by a detached section of 82nd Field Ambulance. Accommodation sleeping for approx 25 sick at present. To left where will take a further 20. Tents being made for available hutting for a convalescent Rest- So far without success. In O. district a very difficulty of large institutional buildings is also very heavily badly provided. On the batchelor talking for inspection of Brigade Sanitary Section consisting of 1 N.C.O. and 25 others per Brigade & formed chiefly of the men who are unfit for trench duty. The general state of sanitary conditions in this area is very bad indeed owing to (1) Permanent sanitary measures of district (2) Recent extremely wet weather (3) Condition of troops. Filthiness in which billets were in being — evacuated by the French.	III

WAR DIARY
or
INTELLIGENCE SUMMARY.
(Erase heading not required.)

Army Form C. 2118.

Hour, Date, Place	Summary of Events and Information	Remarks and references to Appendices
10th Jan 1915. Boeschepe.	Sick Other Ranks 49. WOUNDED. Officers 1 Other Rank 10. Orders issued that Field Ambulances will not change area with Brigades – cancels part of Routine Operation Order No 3. Bedding received for detachment of Supplies unit. very long route marches, Communication with unit very long march march. Orders issued by No 1 that the field hospital to be dispatched without much inconvenience by an officer. Returned Sunday afternoon. duly strafed. A.F. B213 and B531 and B32 with exception of following pp. 51st field amb who could not get away through to 9th and supplies or rather received mainly ill battle. Supplies not rather received mainly ill battle. B.M.S. & Army Printed H.Q.M.S. and reinforced as Brigade Baths and staff house.	[signature] Marshman
11th Jan 1915. Boeschepe.	Sick Officers 3 (Chaplain) Other Ranks 100 Wounded Other Ranks 6 — 80th Brigade returned to the trenches by Plat Bois last night – Large number of the former men were to march over to Dickebusch and a still greater number were unable to get beyond Dickebusch (Brulo) they billeted being about 8 to 9 mile in the rear. The total men unfit on account of feet. But's and sore feet is enormous; this is attributed mainly to the fact, that the Brigade marched in the 9th had some 15 to 16 mile into the trenches.	

WAR DIARY
or
INTELLIGENCE SUMMARY.
(Erase heading not required.)

Army Form C. 2118.

Hour, Date, Place	Summary of Events and Information	Remarks and references to Appendices

11th Continued

The roads were very bad and in many cases the cars came away from the upper. We therefore most of them at rest for two days in every deep mud, in some cases up to the knees. Instructions were issued for Motor Brigades to institute a daily tour of their Brigade area to bring in daily sick from Bulls. It is practically impossible with the present state of the roads and our traffic and ricochets to undertake (?) to evacuate our own sick with our own transport, and free use of the Motor Ambulance Convoy will be made in future. Also Motor Ambulances often to be unavailable for night work in Clearing Sick from the trenches and at the Field Ambulance at these Field Ambulances have been ordered to be kept with the Ambulance in Advance.

Tonight large numbers of men unable to march are distributed about the country between here and DICKEBUSCH and cannot be got at. Reserve Brigade area Troops are collected in BOESCHEPE capable of dealing with some 50 patients.

17th Jan 1915
BOESCHEPE

Sick officers 6 Other Ranks 133. Wounded Other Ranks 8. Bathing Establishment started work today, as far as bathing is concerned saturating and can deal with 100 men per hour changing

[Signature] Maj [?]

Stamp: A.D.M.S. 27th DIVISION

WAR DIARY or INTELLIGENCE SUMMARY

Army Form C. 2118.

Hour, Date, Place	Summary of Events and Information	Remarks and references to Appendices
Th. Jan 15 Cont'd	and washing of underclothes owing to lack of supplies by ordnance and local accommodation in workhouse. Sick – 90% of which are trivial bite and sore feet. Following on a dispatch to Brigade which should have reached here last night, hospital tended to the uttermost and transport of all dis-employees is being used to abring of the sick.	
13th Jan. 15 Boeschepe.	Sick Officers 1 Other Ranks 29, Wounded Other Ranks 16. Mil. The total case of trench bite and swollen feet is considerably more than was anticipated. It totals six thousand to date quite 95% out feet cases. The contributing causes are – long march to trenches as much as 17 miles in some cases on very bad roads – bad boots – dreadful condition of the trenches – long stay in the trenches, in the case of the K.R.C. 72 hours – and the fact that it was their first time in the trench and very few, if any, fit men had passed before being sent into the trenches. It has been decided to form within the resting area a Convalescent Battalion – where men who are not yet fit to go back to the trenches may rest an extra period – This should materially help to reduce the incidence of trench case to hoped.	

F Maurice name

WAR DIARY
or
INTELLIGENCE SUMMARY
(Erase heading not required.)

Army Form C. 2118.

Hour, Date, Place	Summary of Events and Information	Remarks and references to Appendices
14th Jan. 1915. Boeschepe	Sick & Wounded. Officers 3 Other Ranks 303. Wounded officers 1, Other Ranks 14. Divnl. Sanitary Section reported arrival under Command of Lt. White — consisting of 25 N.C.Os. and Men. Range aid Will at present be retained at in the Boeschepe Area. Visit of Bmd.Snr.Army. and Dtr. H.Q. O Boul.	IV
15th Jan. 1915. Boeschepe.	Sick & Wounded Officers 3, Other Ranks 203. Wounded Officers nil other Ranks 20. Estd. Number of sick cases in 80th Brigade from trenches amounts to 570 — (includes wounded also). 6 & 3 made up as follows 2nd K.S.L.I. 165 — 3rd K.R.R.C. 329. 4th K.R.R.C. 369. 4th Rifle Bde. 107. + P.P.L. I. 43., the remainder the several numbers of P.P.C.L.I. Action not yet apparent. Orders issued for formation of Collecting Sin. at Dickebusch to take within intermediate Rdg. Posn. in order to catch as many cases as possible and evacuate them to BAILLEUL before they get so far back as BOESCHEPE which is 9 miles from the firing line. Bathing Establishment at BOESCHEPE as worked as far with satisfactory result, but there is now threatened danger in shortage of water supply. Convd. Ambulances found to work better for collecting the sick at the front. J. Murrenneall Major

WAR DIARY or INTELLIGENCE SUMMARY

Army Form C. 2118.

Hour, Date, Place	Summary of Events and Information	Remarks and references to Appendices
16th Jan 1915. BOESCHEPE	Sick state: Officers 7. Other Ranks 155. Wounded: Officers 3. Other Ranks 15. Visit of Sir Anthony Bowlby and his colleague Henrigton (Specialist Physician & Surgeon to K. Edw.) who handed me a letter over the signed one of Sir John's chaplain to be conveyed — therefore further names of the Cambrai Battalion will have to be taken up today. Sick Isolation Station established in Convent School at WESTOUTRE to work under Bengal Area ambulance direct to Casualty Clearing Station. Most of Division has been very much infected and sick show an undershown under tonsitis & typhoid. Sick state: Officers 7. Other Ranks 106. Wounded Officers 3. Other Ranks 13.	IV
17th Jan 1915. BOESCHEPE	Showers thunder partially answers by use of water carts. Reported some annual amounts. 1 Royal Scot and 1 R.F.A. — of first line to evidence of Epidemiological probably contacted which on leave at home. R. to Cox camp from a horse near DICKEBUSCH when inhabitants are anxious and steps are being taken to seritals return but removal of Contacts with these hearses	

WAR DIARY
or
INTELLIGENCE SUMMARY.
(Erase heading not required.)

Army Form C. 2118.

Hour, Date, Place	Summary of Events and Information	Remarks and references to Appendices
17th Jan 1915. World	Unlikely to be to Corps Dy DMS visited front Area and went round with Cavalry Parties by night.	
18th Jan 1915. Boeschepe.	Sick state officers 5, other Ranks 179 Wounded officers 3 other Ranks 8 Two Motor Lorries Cars changed for two Limbers and two Ford Cars. State of the weather renders sanitation extremely difficult. Brigade sanitary sections are now beginning to work and camouflaged amount of manure is being cleared as well as large accumulations of refuse in and around billets. Facilities of freezing will not permit same to be buried, and a large amount of dumping is only means of disposal, incinerators are being built, and trench latrines on being provided above. The Bde. Sanitary Sections are now permanently instructed in their Area and Sanitary Officer on the Staff of District Commander.	III
19th Jan 1915. Boeschepe.	Sick state officers 5, other Ranks 182 Wounded officers 1, other Ranks 57 A large number of cases Pyrexia in Brigade now occurring, the only apparent cause being the continued cold and wet weather.	

WAR DIARY or INTELLIGENCE SUMMARY

Army Form C. 2118.

Hour, Date, Place	Summary of Events and Information	Remarks and references to Appendices
20th Jan 1915 Boeschepe	Sick officers 4 Other Ranks 155. Wounded officers — Other Ranks 10. Report from Lieut. Col. Buckle (Rifle Brigade) who is being Brigade Commander to which he and 6 days in the Front and 6 days in the reserve area may be due to frequent reliefs within the arrangement appear to be the best that can be managed for resting. Area the officers of the Coy & Bn. Battalion, where men have an easy time and in enjoyment. It however appears to be doubtful; they seem to feel less satisfied and great numbers are going sick. The unhealthy conditions are the principal agent than this cannot be accepted as the cause, however, notice it is operating equally in the other division. Capt. A.H. Nurseries Lambton in the 101 Wessex Coy R.E. attained in a range from hire under observation and kit destroyed. A Motor Car for use of town has been received today. Sick officers 1 Other Ranks 194 Wounded — Other Ranks 12 Disinfectors are being made to establish a Divisional Rest at Boeschepe. Equipment and necessary detail in Boeschepe for Rest Rooms & Rest Lines having obtained. Local picture.	[A.D.M.S. 27th DIVISION stamp] MWMcPherson

WAR DIARY or INTELLIGENCE SUMMARY

Army Form C. 2118.

Hour, Date, Place	Summary of Events and Information	Remarks and references to Appendices
21st Jan '15 (Contd)	Conference held – D.M.S., A.D.M.S., with O/Cs. Field Ambulances were sent down to numbers of sick sent down to unify arrangements. The Officer with the 3 men of Sanitary Coy transferred to DICKEBUSCH for duty. The Sanitary Sections are now working together under Sanitary Officer at DICKEBUSCH where 38 men under Officer at BOESCHEPE where also a certain amount of labour from Composite Battalion – very large accumulation of manure and filth has been dealt with.	
22nd Jan '15 Boeschepe	Sick Officers 8. Other Ranks 235. Wounded Officers 2. Other Ranks 9. 1 O.R. moved DICKEBUSCH – man of 1st Royal Scots – Pte Bridges reported found dead; he had the day before been sent to hospital and while returned as not requiring admission, towards evening no suspicion of want of attendant, possibly a case of decline of his faith. Major Bliss Q.M. Field Ambulance sent to the Divisions temporarily in order to give the benefit of his experience in Field Medical work – sick conditions to improve, thanks in the care of Officers. Eight Ambulances arrived in places of 8 surrendered.	

WAR DIARY
or
INTELLIGENCE SUMMARY.
(Erase heading not required.)

Army Form C. 2118.

Hour, Date, Place	Summary of Events and Information	Remarks and references to Appendices
23rd Jan 1915. Boescheppe	Sick Officers 2 other Ranks 10/6 — Wounded " — " " 1/6 — It has been decided to relieve the 83rd Field Ambulance entirely next week by the 81st Ambulance. It has been arranged to move so that no internal arrangement of sick and wounded takes place internal. Carrying on the actual division etc in the treatment of sick and wounded takes place internal. Kennington reported the arrival in man of A.S.C. attached to 83rd Field Ambulance — the men went sick on the 18th inst. and were complaining to be suffering from foot poisoning — he was transferred to Flenving Hospital on the 19th inst — there are about 40 Cornishes who were sleeping in the same barn — all these have been put under observation and isolated. Sick Officers 2 other Ranks 137/6	
24th Jan 1915. Boescheppe	Wounded " — " " 1/6 — Some sixty to seventy men reporting sick in Rerling Bde and went from Complete Battalion were generally examined and it was found that thirty four were feeling no apparent ailment and were sent to to be were found that thirty four were feeling for light duty in Company and rejoined Battalion. Major Richards came forward to give the benefit of his fresh experience and has formed the 83rd Field Ambulance at DICKEBUSCH	

WAR DIARY or INTELLIGENCE SUMMARY
(Erase heading not required.)

Army Form C. 2118.

Hour, Date, Place	Summary of Events and Information	Remarks and references to Appendices
25th Jan 1915 Boescheepe	Sick Officer 2 Hurbank 95 wounded Other Ranks 8. Lieutenant Kell at Boescheepe and immediately followed — from use of shrapnel in heavy trade in fitting up this hospital. Detailed instructions sent to all units and RMOs as to particular methods to be adopted in order to avoid feedings in men suffering from chilled feet and to 95	V
26th — " —	Sick Officers 3 Other Ranks (3) Wounded — " — 10 Whole of two been received and will be used by Battalion at the rate of 10 gallons to Battalion. Detailed instructions issued to RMOs on the treatment to be adopted in the case of dogs in feet.	VI
27th — " —	Sick Other Ranks 95 Wounded — " — 2 Instructed regard for the use of ventilated equipment. 30 grains of sulphate to be taken by Company of Infantry before the trenches. Platoon Brigade transferred large numbers to each — field camp unable to handle in usual way, this defective to the front. Great numbers of these are obviously to large a number to feed down in Battalions which do not recover as the wounds and to drop in the resting area. Pickepthou are being made to take over another building in Boescheepe to form a second depot.	

Army Form C. 2118.

WAR DIARY
or
INTELLIGENCE SUMMARY.
(Erase heading not required.)

Instructions regarding War Diaries and Intelligence Summaries are contained in F.S. Regs., Part II. and the Staff Manual respectively. Title pages will be prepared in manuscript.

Hour, Date, Place	Summary of Events and Information	Remarks and references to Appendices
27th Jan 1915 Boescheppe Continued	3rd Fld Field Ambulance have now relieved the 2nd Fld Ambulance with the front Amoycana taking over its other billet	
28th Jan 1915	Sick Officers 5 other Ranks 158 Wounded — " 5 Two convoys of evacuated hurts from Officers at Bescheken entrainment service. Late evening — to be removed in the morning. Large auxiliary to be removed in the morning on Gayside Hospital if situation came around to want and of Resting Area Fine weather has changed. In last 3 days - giving the effect on the transfer of greater detail but hand standing. Sick Officers 7 Other Ranks 153 Wounded — " 3 " 30	
29th — " — — " —	Two Officers Batteries from Jeard reported in Div Case of G Causton Spinal Meningitis but Cease of Civilian Statel, who noted this close diagnosis and two Cases of suspected Cerebro Spinal Meningitis, to be Senior, all entirely independently of each other.	J Maurice Maj McEwen

WAR DIARY or INTELLIGENCE SUMMARY

Army Form C. 2118.

Hour, Date, Place	Summary of Events and Information	Remarks and references to Appendices
29th continued	A carried survey of Lambert's Battalion shows 800 obvious sick. My fear is that they are men more than 90% flat cases. Between 30 & 40 cases believed to evacuate and attack the same number fit to rejoin their unit, the remainder requiring 3 to 4 days rest and treatment, the greater proportion probably 10 days.	[A.D.M.S. 27th DIVISION stamp]
30th Jan 1915 Boeschepe	Sick Officer 4 other Ranks 104 Wounded " 5 " 16 Are further cases of cerebro spinal meningitis. Circular memo be more energetic measures to be adopted by R.M.O's.	J Macauliffe Major R.A.M.C.
31st Jan 1915 Boeschepe	Sick Officers 3 other Ranks 36 Wounded " 1 " 9 At REMINGHELST at 10.30 to-day heavy gun manned by batting Bluejackets took place at a range of 11,000 yards. An Analysis of the ack-nowledgments of the end of the month shows the following — Field Ambulances 13-25-26 Admissions. wounded — officer 5? other Ranks 939 294 wounded officers 17, other Ranks 294 sick and accidents cases diagnosed 10. Cerebro spinal cases diagnosed two.	M A Gordon Lt Col R.A.M.C.

INOCULATION RETURN.
27th Division.

UNITS.	Strength. Offrs.	Strength. O.Rks.	Inoculated. Offrs.	Inoculated. O.Rks.	Percentage. Offrs.	Percentage. O.Rks.	Medical Officer.
2nd Shrop.L.I.	27	946	26	943	96.3	99.6	Lt. W.Bell.
3rd K.R.R.Corps.	27	937	20	905	74.07	96.5	Capt.J.M.Williamson.
4th K.R.R.Corps.	28	956	28	956	100.	100.	Lt. J.C.Venniker.
4th R.Brigade.	28	950	28	938	100.	96.5	Lt.J.C.Evatt.
P.P.C.L.Inf.	20	989	20	602	100.	60.8	Maj. C.B.Keenan.
1st R.Scots.	27	1006	27	945	100.	93.9	Lt. O.J.O'Hanlon.
2nd Glester Rgt.	23	781	20	628	72.	80.4	Lt. H.B.Sherlock.
2nd Cameron H.	25	839	25	837	100.	98.8	Capt. B.Biggar.
1st A.& S.Highldrs.	27	982	26	970	96.3	98.7	Lt. G.B.Selby.
1st R.Irish Rgt.	23	863	14	792	60.8	91.7	Lt. E.Phillips.
2nd D.C.L.Inf.	23	929	11	636	48.	68.4	Capt.H.C.Monteith.
2nd R.Irish Fus.	27	857	27	857	100.	100.	Lt. A.P.Brock.
1st Leinster Rgt.	23	900	22	700	95.6	77.7	Lt. C.A.Kenny.
1st Bde R.F.A.	16	457	16	423	100.	92.5	Lt. J.G.Johnson.
15th Bde.R.F.A.	22	745	20	745	90.9	100.	Lt. N.P.Pritchard.
19th Bde.R.F.A.	19	592	19	447	100.	80.	Capt.E.M.Chambers.
20th Bde.R.F.A.	21	603	21	242	100.	40.1	Lt. A.S.Pemberton.
116th Bde.R.G.A.	5	157	5	149	100.	94.9	Lt. N.A.Pritchard.
130th H.Batt.R.F.A.	5	197	5	197	100.	100.	Capt.E.M.Chambers.
Surrey Yeomanry.	6	137	6	132	100.	96.3	82nd Fld.Amb.
Div.Cyclist Coy.	8	199	6	177	75.	88.9	-o- -o- -o-
Div.Engineers.	21	636	20	417	95.2	67.1	Maj.R.O.Stocker.
Div.Signal Coy.	3	97	3	97	100.	100.	-o- -o-
Div.Train A.S.C.	25	607	20	416	80.	68.	Lt. G.B.Forge.
Div.Ammn.Col.	15	339	13	294	86.6	86.7	Capt.H.R.Murison.
16th Mob.Vet.Sec.	1	23	-1-	22	-	95.6	Maj.F.J.Brakenridge.
81st Fld.Amb.	10	239	10	239	100.	100	Lt.Col.J.M.R.Tillston
82nd Fld.Amb.	10	240	10	240	100.	100.	Lt.Col.D.I.Hamilton.
83rd.Fld.Amb.	10	239	7	159	70.	66.07	Lt.Col.G.A.Edsell.
Works Sec.Fld.Ambs.	1	21	1	18	100.	85.7	Maj.F.J.Brakenridge.
Div.Sanitary Sec.	1	23	1	23	100.	100.	Maj.F.J.Brakenridge.
HeadQrs.Unit,27th.Div.	15	70	7	60	46.6	85.7	-o- -o-
	542	17556.	484	15206	89.3	86.6	

Major,
D.A.D.M.S.,
for A.D.M.S.,27th Div.

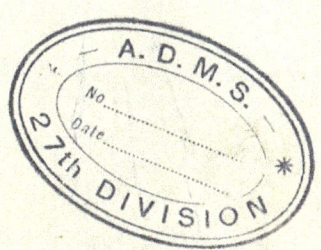

A.D.M.S. 27th Division
Vol II

A.D.M.S. 27th Div. Feb. 1915

Following appx. have been
detached & filed as
under:—

App. I — Re Treatment
of Feet — filed
under "Surgical
Cases" 22(b)

App. II — Re Enteric
Inoculation — filed
under "Enteric"
11(a)

Army Form C. 2118.

"WAR DIARY"
— or —
INTELLIGENCE SUMMARY.
(Erase heading not required.)

Hour, Date, Place	Summary of Events and Information	Remarks and references to Appendices
1st Feb 1915. BOESCHEPE	Sick Males: Officers 3 other Ranks 93 Wounded " 2 " " 3 2nd Field Ambulance moved to RENINGHELST and took over the buildings lately occupied by the 16th French Army Corps — for the present as quarters only.	[A.D.M.S. 27th DIVISION stamp]
2nd	Sick Officers 5 other Ranks 85 Wounded " - " " 13 Brigade Sanitary Squad of Resting Area moved to RENINGHELST, where the sanitary conditions are very bad indeed. Resting of troops is proceeding apace.	
3rd	Sick officers 2 other Ranks 165 Wounded officers Nil — other Ranks 4. Arranged to commence work at Bathing Establishment RENINGHELST — we now have two Bathing Establishments in use — DICKEBUSCH where Battalions Administrative Units and other kit are bathed and the latter refitted with clothing, RENINGHELST where Units in resting area are bathed and refitted and BOESCHEPE where reminder of Brigade in Resting Area is bathed for both purposes. Second Echelon ordered to move to RENINGHELST tomorrow. Bearer Divns. and Field Ambce. required their own Unit. today	[signature] Major R.A.M.C.

WAR DIARY
or
INTELLIGENCE SUMMARY.
(Erase heading not required.)

Army Form C. 2118.

Instructions regarding War Diaries and Intelligence Summaries are contained in F.S. Regs., Part II and the Staff Manual respectively. Title pages will be prepared in manuscript.

Hour, Date, Place	Summary of Events and Information	Remarks and references to Appendices
3rd Feb 1915 BOESCHEPE Contd	Reports as to the use of Whale oil are not very encouraging, the men say if wet the feet colder, and in addition it have a very nauseating odour — the Canadians say it might be useful against warm dampness, but not against cold. D.M.S. 2nd Army visited A.D.M.S today.	
4h "	Sick Officers 7 others 161 Wounded " 1 " 11 Marehouck Convalescent Depot now closed & troops of the Division moved to RENINGHELST.	
5h RENINGHELST	Sick Officers nil others 91 Wounded " 7 " 21 Reported beneficial results from the use of Aquila Ointment — also windproof ointment, the effect of the Ointment being to maintain the circulation of the lower extremities — both being an improvement on Whale oil. A second Convalescent Depot opened at BOESCHEPE — we now have two such Depots and accommodation for about 200 Convalescents in the Division.	J Maberut

WAR DIARY
or
INTELLIGENCE SUMMARY.
(Erase heading not required.)

Army Form C. 2118.

Hour, Date, Place	Summary of Events and Information	Remarks and references to Appendices
6th Feb 1915 RENINGHELST	Sick officers nil others 91 Wounded " 2 " 21 Considerable difficulty is now being experienced in keeping up the supply of toothpicks. It seems now likely however that the crisis is reducing the number of fresh cases.	
7th "	Sick officers nil others 87 Wounded " 9 Instructions received for a contagious ward to be opened in hospital BOESCHEPE for the reception of cases of scabies. Arrangement made for a collecting station to be opened in RENINGHELST, where there are now three battalions quartered, of Rodney Brigade — one battalion at WESTOUTRE. Proceeding post at the latter place to remain for the present as an auxiliary ward.	
8th "	Sick Officers 1 others 130 Wounded 1 " 17 Enteric. There are now 26 cases reported, diagnosed Enteric, in various units. There is no increase in any particular unit. Supplies of whale oil and antiphlebitic great, not being available. A misuse of vaccine has been Forms C. 2118/10— issued. Divisional order published giving J. Mackinnon Mobilization act 16th inst.	

Army Form C. 2118.

WAR DIARY
or
INTELLIGENCE SUMMARY.
(Erase heading not required.)

Instructions regarding War Diaries and Intelligence Summaries are contained in F.S. Regs., Part II and the Staff Manual respectively. Title pages will be prepared in manuscript.

Hour, Date, Place	Summary of Events and Information	Remarks and references to Appendices
9th Feb 15 RENINGHELST	Sick Officers 3 other ranks 93 Wounded " " " 14 The R.O.M.S. inspected a number of reinforcements at BOESCHEPE today and found several even unfit for active service. There is a big leakage of Blankets reported by Infantry Units.	
10th " "	Sick Officers 2 other ranks 111 Wounded " " " 10 O.C. Field Ambulance warned as to their responsibility in keeping a sufficient stock of dressings — having to replenish to M.O. Reports called from the R.M.O's those Units who have returns of those seen of Civilians — to report as to whether any connection between their cases and investigate history of all men engaged in cooking or preparation of food and suspend those who have had enteric. Question has arisen as to disposal of Olives in excess of schedule with the Medical Units on receiving the order to have arrangements All acting whole accordingly	Multiword

WAR DIARY
or
INTELLIGENCE SUMMARY.
(Erase heading not required.)

Army Form C. 2118.

Hour, Date, Place	Summary of Events and Information	Remarks and references to Appendices
11.46 Dec 15/ RENINGHELST	Sick officers 1 other ranks 8. wounded " 1 " " 10	
12" "	Sick officers 3 other ranks 62 wounded " " " 21	
	DICKEBUSCH — man of 4th R. Rifles Bde. removed to BAILLEUL. Rutifraghide frame has now arrived. Report of an outfit of newer France. Generally agree that an improvement in incidence of frost cases has resulted since their use, but as condition of trenches has improved at the same time it is difficult to estimate exact degree due to aid etc.	M. Mahoney
13" — " — "	Sick officers 4 other ranks 66 wounded " 1 " " 8 Arrangements in disposal of patients shown in excess of establish in R.I. stations in units. No new to us now have two convalescent R.I. stations. It is arranged that all equipment belonging to such ambulances which is not at all is in No 1 and all surplus equipment both from British Red Cross Society and Ordnance be ...	

(73989) W4141—463. 400,000. 9/14. H.&J. Ltd. Forms/C. 2118/10.

WAR DIARY
or
INTELLIGENCE SUMMARY.
(Erase heading not required.)

Army Form C. 2118.

Hour, Date, Place	Summary of Events and Information	Remarks and references to Appendices
13th Month	No 3. By order to move patients will be (A) Returned to Units – (B) Evacuated (C) sent to No 2. where they will be evacuated later unless it is possible to leave sufficient personnel in charge. The Equipment will then be envelope for loading in Field Ambulance Transport till at one place.	Manning
	Sick Officers 1 other Rank 82 " 9	
14th	Casualties to then Divisions now amount to 443 cases, but there is still no single front in any Unit, sufficient to point to a carrier or other cause. Many of the R.M.O.'s of corps near of Dunkirk, where by the Engineers at St ELOI. Wells are in hand to improve a Water distilling plant in the brewery at DICKEBUSCH where by very slight adaption the existing plant may be made to distillage by steam about 1000 gallons per day. An attack by Enemy on our trenches repulsed at 5 pm. Sd: Yzer ambulances who are a bit unfixed again were asked it they required help suppliments

WAR DIARY
or
INTELLIGENCE SUMMARY.
(Erase heading not required.)

Army Form C. 2118.

Hour, Date, Place	Summary of Events and Information	Remarks and references to Appendices
15th. Feb. 15. Reninghelst:-	Sick. Officers 2 other Ranks 100 " 3 " 93 Wounded. The extra wounded are part of yesterdays casualties. Third Denrfecator arrived at Boescheppe from D.M.S. Two extra Medical Officers detailed to assist in opening Sliding Station DICKEBUSCH.	
16th. "	Sick. Officers 2 other Ranks 177 " 3 " 49 Wounded. Dressing Station at DICKEBUSCH not opening adequate for given disposal of wounded. Had two days arrangement made to add one hut and increase accommodation & surgical work.	
17th. "	Sick. officers Nil other Ranks 146 " 1 " 30 Wounded. Dressing Bac Linger Ok — arrangement made to have up stock from Riding Ambulance in case of need. by keeping them in halte. 1/3 ready - 1/3 in reserve + 1/3 in use, and all available Ambulance can 1/6 Ambulance in advance.	Attachment JMAdam

WAR DIARY or INTELLIGENCE SUMMARY

Army Form C. 2118.

(Erase heading not required.)

Hour, Date, Place	Summary of Events and Information	Remarks and references to Appendices
18th Feb. 15 Reninghelst	Sick, Officers 1 other ranks 122 Wounded " - " " 22 Inghelsom moved for this Medical Officers to be detailed from Field Ambulance in Resting Area to assist with sick & wounded in front area and be relieved weekly. On report, arrangements in emergency when the Resting Brigade is moved up? The front under emergency two or more other Medical Officers from Resting Area will be detailed by P.M.S. to report to O.C. Field Ambulance in advance. Field Ambulances in Resting Area send at Boescheepe to immediately despatch all available Motor Amb. to front Area to Convalescent Red Chs Beesscheepe. On front Area O.C. Convalescent Red Chs will arrange of furnivous convoy (by application for Motor lorry) to evacuate the more serious cases so as to make room and well not keep more than 200 cases in all in the Red stations. Division order published & promulgated. Instruction & rendering of a monthly state of inoculation put old and offices for transfer to home establishments.	

Army Form C. 2118.

WAR DIARY
or
INTELLIGENCE SUMMARY.
(Erase heading not required.)

Instructions regarding War Diaries and Intelligence Summaries are contained in F.S. Regs., Part II and the Staff Manual respectively. Title pages will be prepared in manuscript.

Hour, Date, Place	Summary of Events and Information	Remarks and references to Appendices
19th Dec. 15- RENINGHELST	Sick Officers Nil Other Ranks 152. Wounded " 1 " " 27 To-day and yesterday Cambridgeshire Regt. arrived and were attached to 82nd Inf. Bde. I, 2nd E. Lanc. being billeted at TERDEGHAM. and arrangements have been made for sick to be evacuated to HAZEBROUCK.	
20th Dec 15- "	Sick Officers 7 other ranks 80 Wounded " 1 " " 9 500 Lehe beds arrived to-day and were issued to those Units for trial and report. Indent sent out daily running expenses of the Bathing Establishment on - abolished - being prepared accordingly.	
21st " "	Sick Officers 1 other Ranks 189 Wounded " " 1 " " 15 ." To-day the heavy evacuation of sick is the 16. the clearing out at BOESCHEPE in order to unblock the Rest. Station of the evacuation 5-3- were Rheumatics and 66 Dec: cases	W. Mahenead

Army Form C. 2118.

WAR DIARY
or
INTELLIGENCE SUMMARY.
(Erase heading not required.)

Instructions regarding War Diaries and Intelligence Summaries are contained in F.S. Regs., Part II. and the Staff Manual respectively. Title pages will be prepared in manuscript.

Hour, Date, Place	Summary of Events and Information	Remarks and references to Appendices
22nd Feb 1915. RENINGHELST	Sick Officers 1 other Ranks 61 Wounded " 1 " " 17 Information received that a hospital for scabies: General Spinal Meningitis in established in BAILLEUL.	
23rd Feb 15.	Sick Officers 1 other Ranks 95 Wounded " " " 15 Lt/Col S. Stephenson arrived today.	
24th Feb 15. "	Sick Officers Nil other Ranks 93 Wounded " " " 17	
25th Feb 15. "	Sick Officers 2 other Ranks 99 Wounded " 1 " " 18 Visit of D.M.S. 2nd Army. A case of Cerebro Spinal Meningitis reported in 83rd Field Ambulance, necessary instructions issued re Contacts	

[A.D.M.S. 27th DIVISION stamp]

(73989) W4141—463. 400,000. 9/14. H.&J.Ltd. Forms/C. 2118/10.

WAR DIARY
or
INTELLIGENCE SUMMARY.
(Erase heading not required.)

Army Form C. 2118.

Hour, Date, Place	Summary of Events and Information	Remarks and references to Appendices
26th Feb 1915 RENINGHELST	Sick officers 2 other Ranks 133 wounded " 3 " " 21	
27th " "	Sick officers 1 other Ranks 83 wounded " 1 " " 21	
28th " "	Sick officers 2 other Ranks 72 wounded " 1 " " 1st 9th Royal East arrived today and have been quartered near BOESCHEPE. Typhoid incidence in Division shows a definite falling off by rate — 15—18—12 — 6 — for the four weeks of this month. Many farms are infected but the number of troops now in area is so great that none can be spared. Milk and buttles are out of bounds and water is either all boiled or chlorinated. The together with a new very complete inoculation is hoped to protect us. In the front area beyond DICKEBUSCH undoubtedly, water is	

WAR DIARY
or
INTELLIGENCE SUMMARY.
(Erase heading not required.)

Army Form C. 2118.

Hour, Date, Place	Summary of Events and Information	Remarks and references to Appendices
28th month RENINGHELST.	Chief cause and most of the Regimental Medical Officers inspect water from the Region of ST ELOI as cause of their cases. Arrangements have now been made to supply 10 water Carts full per day of Sterilized (by Steam) and Chlorinated water for use of Units going into the trenches. Chilled feet cases in the town are now a trifle falling off, but average evacuation from the cases on still 28 cases per day. The war job is not very impatient. The men object especially to antiperiodic, please because of it headiness.	[stamp: A.D.M.S. 27th DIVISION] Skeleton in jumper DCA Gordon Lt Colonel ADMS 27th Div

121/4693
March 1915

ADMS. 27th Division

Vol III

ADMS 27th Division

Army Form C. 2118.

WAR DIARY
or
INTELLIGENCE SUMMARY.
(Erase heading not required.)

Hour, Date, Place	Summary of Events and Information	Remarks and references to Appendices
1st March 1915 RENINGHELST	Sick Officers nil other ranks 61 Wounded " 1 " " 37 Heavy casualties due to activity on left sector of trenches. Accumulation of the enemy's dead in front of our trenches has resulted in trenches becoming most insanitary, the bodies cannot at present be buried, owing to exposure to fire, from the front they are being covered with chloride of lime at night. (MS)	[A.D.M.S. 27th DIVISION stamp]
2nd March	Sick Officers nil other ranks 106 Wounded " 1 " " 85 The Motor bus allotted for her has been posted with headquarters Cav Divisional under orders from 27th Division. The D.M.S. been notified. Recent shelling of DICKEBUSCH in causing anxiety in the proximity of Dressing Station, arrangements are in hand to accommodate same in a less dangerous locality, preferably by training of huts. Two Sick Cases were evacuated today (MS) in transit from DICKEBUSCH Dressing Station.	

Army Form C. 2118.

WAR DIARY
or
INTELLIGENCE SUMMARY.
(Erase heading not required.)

[Stamp: A.D.M.S. 27th DIVISION]

Hour, Date, Place	Summary of Events and Information	Remarks and references to Appendices

3rd March /15
RENINGHELST

Sick Officers 3 other ranks 43
Wounded " 5 " 35

Supplies of Paper Stationery, Disinfectant
are expected, all Units have been warned
and instructions issued in anticipation.
Those remaining stakes, squares and
sent down for exchange.
Field Ambulances have been instructed
to give every assistance to Grave Registration
Committee when necessary.

4th March /15

Sick Officers 0 other ranks 129
Wounded " 1 " 21

Advance Depot Medical Stores
now located in POPERINGHE that informed.

5th March /15

Sick Officers 1 other ranks 118
Wounded " 1 " 14

Case of Cerebro Spinal Meningitis
occurred at WESTOUTRE, infection ambulance
asked and case sent down to ST OMER, two
contacts sent to isolation hospital BAILLEUL.

Army Form C. 2118.

WAR DIARY
or
INTELLIGENCE SUMMARY.
(Erase heading not required.)

Instructions regarding War Diaries and Intelligence Summaries are contained in F.S. Regs., Part II and the Staff Manual respectively. Title pages will be prepared in manuscript.

Hour, Date, Place	Summary of Events and Information	Remarks and references to Appendices
5th March '15 (contd)	Paper sleeping bags now been received and issued by Commandant. DICKEBUSCH in proportion of 2000 to each Brigade in front area, an early report being asked for. A.D.M.S. visits Regimental Aid Posts at VE MOZELE.	[stamp: A.D.M.S. 27th DIVISION]
6th March '15	Sick officers 1 other ranks 75 Wounded " 1 " 25 ENTERIC — we now have 62 cases in the Division, but there is still no evidence of grouping. Some cases are distributed. Headqrs 27th Division asked to assist re low percentage of other rank inoculated in 1st D.C.L.I. and 20th Bde R.F.A. Divisional order re supply of drinking water No 7 of 6.3.15	J.W.

Army Form C. 2118.

WAR DIARY
or
INTELLIGENCE SUMMARY.
(Erase heading not required.)

Instructions regarding War Diaries and Intelligence Summaries are contained in F.S. Regs., Part II. and the Staff Manual respectively. Title pages will be prepared in manuscript.

Hour, Date, Place	Summary of Events and Information	Remarks and references to Appendices
7th March RENINGHELST.	Sick officers 3 other ranks 77 Wounded " 2 " " 22 Lt. A.T. Shropshires Medical officer wounded left buttock. wounded today, Shrapnel Claim for 2,900 Francs compensation received from owner of Brewery DICKEBUSCH. that is being used as a Bathing Establishment this Division — this has been forwarded to Headqrs 27th Divn for consideration.	[stamp: A.D.M.S. 27th DIVISION]
8th March '15	Sick officers 1 other ranks 81 wounded " - " " 23 Excellent report received from Brigade on the use of Water front Paper stockings — Unit having used them where they kept men's feet warm and dry — D.M.S. informed of result by wire. Brigade are being carried at DICKEBUSCH for bath during chest for AM.	

(73989) W.4141—463. 400,000. 9/14. H.&J.Ltd. Forms/C. 2118/10.

Army Form C. 2118.

WAR DIARY
or
INTELLIGENCE SUMMARY.
(Erase heading not required.)

Instructions regarding War Diaries and Intelligence Summaries are contained in F.S. Regs., Part II and the Staff Manual respectively. Title pages will be prepared in manuscript.

Hour, Date, Place	Summary of Events and Information	Remarks and references to Appendices
9th March '15 RENINGHELST	Sick officers Nil other ranks 92. Wounded " 1 " 15 A.D.M.S. wants to prepare for heavy casualties. Field Ambulances in advance ordered to evacuate all sick and wounded, supplies of Dressings & bandages prepared for despatch by Field Ambulances in advance. Extra medical officers sent forward to army. G.O.C. has decided to abolish the Composite Battalions — this will mean a great increase in evacuation of sick. As men become fit for duty they will be returned to duty until all have been disposed of — no more cases being sent in.	[27th DIVISION A.D.M.S. stamp]
10th March '15	Sick officers 5 other ranks 70 Wounded " — " 13 2nd Field Ambulance relieved 3rd on the front area and return to Bullets. Treated by Sqd in reserve area. Taken book in each case not to be left in the relieving party has taken over — Relief duties cannot....	OM.

Army Form C. 2118.

WAR DIARY
or
INTELLIGENCE SUMMARY.
(Erase heading not required.)

Instructions regarding War Diaries and Intelligence Summaries are contained in F.S. Regs., Part II. and the Staff Manual respectively. Title pages will be prepared in manuscript.

Hour, Date, Place	Summary of Events and Information	Remarks and references to Appendices
11th March 15" RENINGHELST	Sick officers 1 other ranks 84 Wounded " — " 18 Informed to-day that operations performed by Field Ambulance not successful owing in many cases to weather being deferred at Casualty Clearing Stations or base. Field Ambulances are not to perform such operations except where necessary to save life.	
13th March 15" "	Sick officers Nil other ranks 80 Wounded " " " 2" A.D.S. attended Dranoutre between two cases dressed same on another in infection - all contacts segregated. In the latter case the contacts were exposed out of the trenches and brought back to reserve area.	
14 March 15" "	Sick officers 2 other ranks 93 Wounded " 1 " 25	

(73989) W4141—463. 400,000. 9/14. H.&J. Ltd. Forms/C. 2118/10.

Army Form C. 2118.

WAR DIARY
or
INTELLIGENCE SUMMARY.
(Erase heading not required.)

Instructions regarding War Diaries and Intelligence Summaries are contained in F.S. Regs., Part II. and the Staff Manual respectively. Title pages will be prepared in manuscript.

Hour, Date, Place	Summary of Events and Information	Remarks and references to Appendices
14 March '15 RENINGHELST.	Sick officers 1 other ranks 73 Wounded " 3 " - Reported personally to G.O.C. 27th Divn concerning occurrences in DICKEBUSCH and neighbourhood, suggested that more lighting places should be obtained in vicinity of LA CLYTTE, or elsewhere, also inference how 7 officers and other ranks evacuated on one date by L.F. and high percentage of venereal incidence in that unit (12 Cavs.)	[stamp: A.D.M.S. 27th DIVISION]
15th March '15	Sick officers nil other ranks 63 Wounded " 4 " 105 Heavy evacuation of wounded. The result of an attack on our front last night. So meet the emergency supplies of bandages & dressings were depleted from Divisional Ambulances, also the assistance of two extra Medical Officers and all available motor ambulances.	JM.

Army Form C. 2118.

WAR DIARY
or
INTELLIGENCE SUMMARY.
(Erase heading not required.)

Instructions regarding War Diaries and Intelligence Summaries are contained in F.S. Regs., Part II. and the Staff Manual respectively. Title pages will be prepared in manuscript.

Hour, Date, Place	Summary of Events and Information	Remarks and references to Appendices
16th March '15 RENINGHELST	Sick officer 1 other rank 92. Wounded officer 9 " " 165. One R.A.M.C. man 63rd Field Ambce (Bearer) wounded last night.	[A.D.M.S. 27th DIVISION stamp]
17th March '15 "	Sick officer 2 other ranks 67 Wounded " 2 " " 65 Headquarters warned as to the probable scarcity of water in this district in near future and suggested construction construction of Dam at one or two points. All water cart of division inspected by sanitary officer who reports that heavy cars are in a bad condition	
18th March '15 "	Sick officer 4 other ranks 67 Wounded " 1 " " 28	JW

Army Form C. 2118.

WAR DIARY
or
INTELLIGENCE SUMMARY.
(Erase heading not required.)

Instructions regarding War Diaries and Intelligence Summaries are contained in F.S. Regs., Part II. and the Staff Manual respectively. Title pages will be prepared in manuscript.

Hour, Date, Place	Summary of Events and Information	Remarks and references to Appendices
19th March /15 RENINGHELST	Sick officers 2 other ranks 50. wounded " 3 " " 45.	[A.D.M.S. 27th DIVISION stamp]
20th March 15	Sick officers 2 other ranks 46 wounded " 1 " " 36.	
21st March 15	Sick officers 2 other ranks 103 wounded " — " " 21	
22nd March	Sick officers 1 other ranks 767 wounded " 1 " " 35 Heavy evacuation due to emptying Composite Batns & Convalescent Ret. in preparation of Divisions moving. Bearing & Divisional Detachment Closed. Equipment & detachment ordered to rejoin their unit. 2nd Field Ambulance	
23rd March '15	Sick officers 2 other ranks 193 wounded " 1 " " 18 Continue heavy evacuation th balance of yesterday clear up. Preliminary operation order received	JMS

Army Form C. 2118.

WAR DIARY
or
INTELLIGENCE SUMMARY.
(Erase heading not required.)

Instructions regarding War Diaries and Intelligence Summaries are contained in F.S. Regs., Part II. and the Staff Manual respectively. Title pages will be prepared in manuscript.

[Stamp: A.D.M.S. 27th DIVISION]

Hour, Date, Place	Summary of Events and Information	Remarks and references to Appendices
23rd March '15 RENINGHELST.	Field Ambulances attached to Brigades and come under orders of G.O.C. Brigades in regard moves. 1st with 2nd Brigade, 2nd with 81st Brigade & 3rd with 80th Brigade.	
24th March '15	Sick officers 2 other ranks 62. Wounded " 1 " 18 Arrangements made with 2nd Division re collecting sick, wounded for casualties during proposed change of duty of 27th Division. 81st Field Ambulance relieved by 8th Field Ambulance today, the former returning to billets in RENINGHELST. Sanitary Section now back to BOESCHEPE, most of their equipment lost in Bathing Establishment RENINGHELST.	
25th March '15	Sick officers 2 other ranks 23 Wounded " - " 1 D.A.D.M.S. inspects VLAMERTINGHE wrt report unfavourably upon its fitness for occupation by our troops. The village found to be in a very unsanitary condition, water supply dangerous.	AMS

WAR DIARY
or
INTELLIGENCE SUMMARY.
(Erase heading not required.)

Army Form C. 2118.

Hour, Date, Place	Summary of Events and Information	Remarks and references to Appendices
25th Continued	Period two being collected from all units for the purpose of being used to carry water up to the trenches.	[27th Division stamp]
26th March RENINGHELST	Sick officer — other ranks 13.	
	Division now practically relieved and units centred about the district noted.	
27th March 15	Sick officer 1 other ranks 16. All R.M.O wanted to take advantage of the lulling period. Progress agreed on. Inoculation against Enteric. S.O. to ask for an experimental to be made with the Beresh Malamak Carriage, Ambulance, Artichoken. Three authorised for as a trial.	
28th	Sick other ranks 19	A.M.
29th	Sick officers 6 other ranks 7	

WAR DIARY or INTELLIGENCE SUMMARY.

(Erase heading not required.)

Army Form C. 2118.

Instructions regarding War Diaries and Intelligence Summaries are contained in F.S. Regs., Part II. and the Staff Manual respectively. Title pages will be prepared in manuscript.

Hour, Date, Place	Summary of Events and Information	Remarks and references to Appendices
30th March/15. RENINGHELST	Sick officers Nil other ranks 21. 83rd Field Ambulance move to Billets in a farm 2 miles east of Poperinghe on the Boeschepe road.	[stamp: A.D.M.S. 27th DIVISION]
31st March/15. RENINGHELST	Sick officers 4 other ranks 14. Evacuation to R.M.O. is evacuation of sick or wounded through Channels other than the Field Ambulance, also to take advantage of opportunities to send sick men to all ranks to First-Aid & the use of Field Dressings & shell dressings. All R.M.O.s warned re accumulation of sick, especially those unable to march in view of orders to move at ———. Enemy's Casualties as reported. To date 91 cases have been reported of the Unit (2nd Dt.L.I.) having the largest percentage of officers & others inoculated, has had the highest number of cases – 15.	J Shewsmith Lt Colonel D.D.M.S. 27th Div. C C Gibson A.D.M.S. 27th Div. and Division

121/5257
April 1915

examined but not copied
25/4/17

121/5251

A.D.M.S. 27th Division

Vol IV

WAR DIARY or INTELLIGENCE SUMMARY

Army Form C. 2118.

Hour, Date, Place	Summary of Events and Information	Remarks and references to Appendices
1st April 1915 RENINGHELST.	Sick. Officers & other ranks 18 Wounded. YPRES. Sanitary Section proceed to Billets in YPRES. O.C. 82nd & 83rd Fd. Ambs. undertook to arrange that the latter furnish rations for patients heavy dept. behind at Divisional Rest Station when the former move off. That Field Ambulances proceed to YPRES and make preparations to receive wounded at College Episcopal, also sick from Front area, and are cross Censure Officer meninghi on PPDLD.	JM
2nd April 15 "	Sick officers 5 other ranks 45. Wounded Nil. Divisional order published re demarking water new area. Letter conveying instructions in re Laundries about 30 contacts segregated. 8 Brigade relieved on night of near area. Vavin wells inspected near trenches in new area.	I JM

WAR DIARY or INTELLIGENCE SUMMARY.

Army Form C. 2118.

(Erase heading not required.)

Hour, Date, Place	Summary of Events and Information	Remarks and references to Appendices
3rd April '15 RENINGHELST.	Sick officers 1 other ranks 55. Wounded Nil Circular letter to Regimental Medical officers and Units that war can must be taken to prevent wastage and reduce evacuation of slight cases. Two contacts for Cerebro Spinal Meningitis in P.P.C.L.I. to be sent to Isolation Hospital BAILLEUL for examination as personal contacts. No wounded during first night in new trenches.	II AM
4th April '15 "	Sick officers Nil other ranks 21 Wounded " " " 23 3rd. Brigade relieved in left section. No new area. 2nd Field Ambulance and balance of Sanitary Section moved to Bulsk. in YPRES, less personnel left with No 2 Rest Station BOESCHEPE. Collecting Sta. WESTOUTRE closed.	AM

Army Form C. 2118.

WAR DIARY
or
INTELLIGENCE SUMMARY.
(Erase heading not required.)

Instructions regarding War Diaries and Intelligence Summaries are contained in F.S. Regs., Part II. and the Staff Manual respectively. Title pages will be prepared in manuscript.

Hour, Date, Place	Summary of Events and Information	Remarks and references to Appendices
5th April '15 RENINGHELST YPRES	Sick officers Nil other ranks 14. Wounded " " " 15. Headquarters 27th Division (including A.D. M.S.) moved to YPRES. Advanced Headqrs established at POTIJZE. Difficulty in arranging disposition owing to frequent changes in the area allotted to Division. Inspected various Aid Posts	JMcC
6th April '15 YPRES	Sick officers 4 other ranks 8 Wounded " — " " 27 Som. Light Ambulance began to move from ECOLE Payart to Civil Hospital.	JMcC
7th April '15 "	Sick officers Nil other ranks 31 Wounded " 1 " " 31. 80th Brigade moved into different area. Collecting post released by Brigade accepted for temporary use, but an expedition found to be inconveniently placed. Had Capt B. Biggar M.O. to 1st Leinsters sent down sick. We are now seven M.O.'s short of Establishment. 5 of whom are unlikely to return	JMcC

Army Form C. 2118.

WAR DIARY
or
INTELLIGENCE SUMMARY.
(Erase heading not required.)

Hour, Date, Place	Summary of Events and Information	Remarks and references to Appendices
8th April '15 YPRES	Sick officers 1 other ranks 19 Wounded " - " 38 Kit pack needed in right section, ammunition that wanted in the section may be got out in daylight. 83rd Field Ambulance move from Billet south of POPERINGHE to G 11 a 1/40000 Belgian map, South of POPERINGHE – VLAMERTINGHE road, to occupy two farms.	AMS
9th April '15 "	Sick officers 1 - 38 Wounded " - 29 Three stretcher carriage ambulances received per train to truck in front area. Bevan McCormack received for first to truck in front area. 3rd Field Ambulance move into CIVIL HOSPITAL - YPRES and prepare to receive light cases from the front area and the sick from this. Divisional Rest-Station No 3 BOESCHEPE now closed up, the remaining 70 Casis. 5.8 have been transferred to HAZEBROUCK No 10 B.E. Station & is relieved by duty.	AMS

Army Form C. 2118.

WAR DIARY
or
INTELLIGENCE SUMMARY.
(Erase heading not required.)

Hour, Date, Place	Summary of Events and Information	Remarks and references to Appendices
10th April/15 YPRES	Sick officers 3 other ranks 9 Wounded " 1 " 33	
	Sick — officers 1 other ranks 16 Wounded " — " " — Orders received to send one field Ambulance out of YPRES to relieve congestion in billeting area. 82nd Fd. Amb. left via Zonn L'EBBE west of POPERINGHE & the 8 2nd Fd. Amb. relieved them at Farm on a route of POPERINGHE – VLAMERTINGHE road	JW
11th April/15 "	Sick officers 1 other ranks 16 Wounded " — " " 41	JW
12th April/15 "	Sick officers — other ranks — Wounded " " " 82nd Field Ambulance took for a Divisional Rest Station and fitted tents at L'EBBE Farm 3 Bearer McDonnell Hitchen, Conroy, ambulance turned to regimental aid post	JW

Army Form C. 2118.

WAR DIARY
or
INTELLIGENCE SUMMARY.
(Erase heading not required.)

Instructions regarding War Diaries and Intelligence Summaries are contained in F.S. Regs., Part II and the Staff Manual respectively. Title pages will be prepared in manuscript.

Hour, Date, Place	Summary of Events and Information	Remarks and references to Appendices
13th April '15 YPRES	Sick officers – other ranks 13 Wounded " " 3 " 33 3rd Field Ambulance, many comforts and the extra equipment left at BOESCHEPE. Rest Station has now been taken over at L'EBBE Farm. 2nd Field Ambulance moved two sections to new quarters. First day of new system of collecting wounded in two heavy lorries at dusk and dawn is working very well. Seems a gain from all point of view. Supply of oxygen has been obtained and sent up to trenches in the event of P.S. Mines being used. Accommodation now available at MT de CATS for eighty sick officers who are likely to recover with a week or ten days.	[stamp: A.D.M.S. 27th DIVISION] JM

Army Form C. 2118.

WAR DIARY
or
INTELLIGENCE SUMMARY.
(Erase heading not required.)

Instructions regarding War Diaries and Intelligence Summaries are contained in F.S. Regs., Part II. and the Staff Manual respectively. Title pages will be prepared in manuscript.

Hour, Date, Place	Summary of Events and Information	Remarks and references to Appendices
14th April 15 YPRES.	Sick officers 1 other Ranks 37 Wounded " — " 19 Bearer McCormack stretcher reports very useful, three more have been applied for. 58 Patients being sent to Canadian Red Cross Station HAZEBROUCK as L'EBBE Farm not yet available. Previous steps have been undertaken for use of R.Eng. at Regimental Aid Posts.	M
15th April 15 YPRES.	Sick officers NIL other Ranks 35 Wounded " — " 13 Warned to prepare for probable attack as to casualties. Bearer Division of 8nd Field Ambulance brought up to render assistance if required and arrangements made to accommodate patients in Civil hospital under canvas, west of POPERINGHE — to conn A Divisional Red Station opened admitting from YPRES	M

WAR DIARY
or
INTELLIGENCE SUMMARY.
(Erase heading not required.)

Army Form C. 2118.

Hour, Date, Place	Summary of Events and Information	Remarks and references to Appendices
16th April '15 YPRES	Sick 14 otherwise 30 wounded " Major I.A. Peyton R.A.M. appointed Sanitary Officer YPRES O.C. 2nd Field Ambulance ordered to send two N.C.O.s & ten men to be attached to 3rd Fd Ambulance in reserve. These N.C.O & men to learn the collecting area in advance to be relieved weekly	JW
17th April '15 YPRES	Sick officers 1 otherwise 29 Wounded " " 34 Lieut Delgado evacuated sick Relieved by Capt H. Fallin R.A.M.C. Att 2nd Field Amb.	JW
18th April '15 YPRES	Sick officers — otherwise 30 Wounded " 1 " 45 Lieut W. Bell R.A. no. 1 to 2nd Fd. Ambulance slightly wounded. Bullet thro' right leg, continued duty. Lieut Price, R.V. Dunn, P. Mathew and J.P. Mitchell arrive as reinforcement YPRES shelled	JW

WAR DIARY
or
INTELLIGENCE SUMMARY.
(Erase heading not required.)

Army Form C. 2118.

Hour, Date, Place	Summary of Events and Information	Remarks and references to Appendices
19th April '15 YPRES	Sick officers 2 other ranks 23 Wounded " " " 34 Lieut. Roy & G. Stocker, M.O. of Divisional Engineers slightly wounded (shrapnel) head YPRES again shelled, the chief officer being one of the casualties - the casualties to-day from shelling being 6 other ranks killed and 3 officers and 36 other ranks wounded. Officer of RD MS gave to a man of Kemmes Station A Coy. near MENIN Gate	JW
20th April '15 YPRES	Sick other ranks 23 Wounded " 72 YPRES again shelled, many casualties being admitted by No 3 Ld Amb[ulance]. Very heavy fighting at Hill 60. Sick officers of AD MS knocked by two shells.	
21st April '15 YPRES	Sick officer 5 other ranks 20 Wounded " 1 " 66 YPRES shelled up to 8 a.m. — commencing again during the evening. Administrative HQrs moved to POTYSE. Heavy fighting continued at Hill 60.	JW

Army Form C. 2118.

WAR DIARY
or
INTELLIGENCE SUMMARY.
(Erase heading not required.)

Instructions regarding War Diaries and Intelligence Summaries are contained in F. S. Regs., Part II and the Staff Manual respectively. Title pages will be prepared in manuscript.

Hour, Date, Place	Summary of Events and Information	Remarks and references to Appendices
22nd April/15 YPRES	Sick officers 4 other ranks 9 Wounded " 1 " 17 Heavy shelling of YPRES continued throughout the day MENIN BRIDGE close by one of the chief targets. GERMAN attack north of YPRES began	M
23rd April/15 YPRES	Sick officers NIL other ranks 19/ Wounded " " " 36 Heavy shelling, especially during the morning. Office of A.D.M.S. moved out of YPRES to POPERINGHE. Very heavy casualties. 2 Bearers 3rd Field Ambulance killed during night and 1 officer Capt. H.S. Kollen wounded.	M
24th April/15 POPERINGHE.	Sick other ranks 4 Wounded " " 22 Warned to expect heavy casualties. Canadians heavily engaged. POPERINGHE shelled at 9-10 A.M. 36 Bearers and 6 cars lent to Canadian Divn at other times all day evacuating wounded this Corps in new firing line being developed.	M

(73989) W4141—463. 400,000. 9/14. H.&J.Ltd. Forms/C. 2118/10.

Army Form C. 2118.

WAR DIARY
or
INTELLIGENCE SUMMARY.
(Erase heading not required.)

Instructions regarding War Diaries and Intelligence Summaries are contained in F.S. Regs., Part II and the Staff Manual respectively. Title pages will be prepared in manuscript.

Hour, Date, Place	Summary of Events and Information	Remarks and references to Appendices
25th April '15 POPERINGHE	Sick officers 7 other ranks 17. Wounded " 9 " 139 HOOSE bearers did not get back until about 9 am. Shells began again in POPERINGHE at about 3pm. Extra Bearer Party ½ a Sec Coy sent out to help on POTYSE bus line at 2 am.	M
26th April '15 POPERINGHE	Sick officers 1 other ranks 17 Wounded " 1 " 95 Headquarters visited at POTYSE — our own divisional Area not heavily engaged, did numbers of casualties other divisions sent with — chiefly Canadian Division. Office of A.D.M.S. again worked day & Nt. — Transferred to L'EBBE Farm with 82nd 2Cd.F. Ambulance 48 men fit for duty from Divisional Rest Station sent up to trenches with our Bearer Party	M

A.D.M.S. 27th DIVISION

(73989) W4141—463. 400,000. 9/14. H.&J.Ltd. Forms/C. 2118/10.

WAR DIARY
or
INTELLIGENCE SUMMARY.
(Erase heading not required.)

Army Form C. 2118.

Instructions regarding War Diaries and Intelligence Summaries are contained in F.S. Regs., Part II and the Staff Manual respectively. Title pages will be prepared in manuscript.

Hour, Date, Place	Summary of Events and Information	Remarks and references to Appendices
27th April '15 LEBBE Farm POPERINGHE	Sick officers NIL other ranks 40. Wounded " 3 " " 94. Reserves are now being sent from the three Field Ambulances in rotation so as to keep each unit fresh and ready. Motor Drivers very fatigued as their work is practically incessant.	JM
28th April '15 LEBBE Farm	Sick & wounded last night (#1) from (HOOGE) evacuated through bolt Dressing Station at VLAMERTINGHE where they are received by Motor Convoy to HAZEBROUCK or BAILLEUL. Seven Motor Ambulances have offered (R. Devonia) sent to 28th Division for road work east of VLAMERTINGHE.	JM
29th April '15 LEBBE Farm	Sick & other ranks wounded evacuated from LEBBE Farm. Comparatively quiet day. 87 cases sick and wounded collected from HOOGE and all evacuated through the bolted Dressing Shd at VLAMERTINGHE. Owing to this arrangement we have no check on the divisional cases, this has been handed over to D.D.M.S. shell hole from Motor Amb. broken by passing our...	JM

Army Form C. 2118.

WAR DIARY
or
INTELLIGENCE SUMMARY.
(Erase heading not required.)

Hour, Date, Place	Summary of Events and Information	Remarks and references to Appendices
30th April '15 LEBBE farm POPERINGHE	Sick officers Nil other Ranks 9 Wounded " " 7 The organization of wounded was today during Battle VLAMERTINGHE from today we commence to collect and evacuate our own Divisional wounded This is done from LEBBE farm 11 miles from the firing line and without difficulty, by means of good roads Ambulances The sick through YPRES is dangerous on account of shell fire. [signature] M.A.Gordon Colonel AMS ADMS 27th Division	[stamp: 27th DIVISION] [signature] Enumerated and signed

Extract from D.O. 3rd April 1915.

1. DRINKING WATER IN TRENCHES. None of the water from walls in the vicinity of the new trenches is fit for drinking direct and untreated. All ranks are forbidden to use this water except for cooking or making tea.

Water for drinking will be carried up (a) in water-bottle on the man (b) in water carts sufficient for refilling bottles once in 24 hours.

This water is to be obtained from the prepared supply at the swimming bath near the MENIN gate at YPRES and from no other place.

It is hoped to provide a supplimentary supply at HOOGE in a few days.

Extract from D.O. 4th April 1915.

3. WATERING HORSES. All horses will be watered from buckets in order to avoid fouling the water supply.

Extract from D.O. 8th April 1915.

6. WATER. Drinking water for use of all Units,- VLAMERTINGHE and its vicinity- will be obtained from the swimming bath at YPRES. The water at VLAMERTINGHE is highly dangerous.

Statistics

Medical Officer i/c

Regt

It is notified for general information that the statistics of sick in this division compare very unfavourably with figures of all other divisions in the Army.

The 27th Division evacuates more than twice as many sick as the average of other divisions, and three or four times as many as some divisions.

The reasons for this disparity are that R M Os in the first place, and Medical Units in the second are not sufficiently strict in dealing with the light cases, and many more than is necessary of these cases are sent to Field Ambulances, and having arrived there many are evacuated that could be made fit for duty by a few days rest and <u>active treatment</u>.

I rely on R.M.Os. to exercise henceforth a much stricter supervision on the cases they send to hospital.

Meanwhile all Medical Units will exercise rigid supervision on the cases evacuated, and whenever extra pains or work can <u>obviate</u> men being evacuated it should be given unstintingly

C.C.A. Gordon
Colonel A.m.s.
A.D.M.S. 27th Division

H.Q., 27th Div.
3rd April '15

121/5609

121/5609

May 1915

examined - not copied 25.9.17

ADMS. 27th Division

Vol VI

Army Form C. 2118.

WAR DIARY
or
INTELLIGENCE SUMMARY.
(Erase heading not required.)

Hour, Date, Place	Summary of Events and Information	Remarks and references to Appendices
1st May 1915 EBBE-FARM POPERINGHE	Sick officers 1 other ranks 6. Wounded " 1 " " 46 Sick and wounded continue to be evacuated from booked Dressing Station at VLAMERTINGHE 81st Field Ambulance move to a Farm on POPERINGHE - RENINGHELST road.	
2nd May '15 " "	Sick officers 4 – other ranks 19 Wounded " 2 " " 46 2nd Field Ambulance established a Dressing Station in Convent, Poerinck, POPERINGHE – Many cases of Asphyxiation admitted, mostly from 4th Division – a state of unrest found to have a very disquieting effect on the troops. A Reference at Doncaster General Convey GS to Medical Units, regarding work carried out in recent operations. YPRES district.	

Army Form C. 2118.

WAR DIARY
or
INTELLIGENCE SUMMARY.
(Erase heading not required.)

Instructions regarding War Diaries and Intelligence Summaries are contained in F.S. Regs., Part II. and the Staff Manual respectively. Title pages will be prepared in manuscript.

Hour, Date, Place	Summary of Events and Information	Remarks and references to Appendices
2nd May 1915. EBBE-FARM	Sick officers Nil other ranks 2. Wounded " 0 " " 2. 81st Field Ambulance ordered to occupy BRANDHOEK School, south of POPERINGHE – VLAMERTINGHE road for general use as our Field Ambulance be brought out to Fort Field Ambulance. Materials received to under 3500. Fresh respirators for use of troops in area where Gas is being used. These are now being made of Gauze & cotton waste damped in thiosulphate solution, in our Divisional Rest Station by the R.A.M.C. men and patients.	(A.D.M.S. stamp 27th Division)
4th May /15. — " —	Sick officers 6 other ranks 82. wounded — " — 2 — " — 149. Heavy casualties in 80th Brigade. Following the move back into fresh trenches mostly deep dugouts. Lt Col. C.M. Rogers Yorkshire Lt. Rgt. Dd. and afterwards Dick – Stricture. J.W. [signature]

WAR DIARY
or
INTELLIGENCE SUMMARY.
(Erase heading not required.)

Army Form C. 2118.

Hour, Date, Place	Summary of Events and Information	Remarks and references to Appendices
4th continued	Capt. H.S. Hollis 82nd Field Ambulance wounded, shrapnel left arm. Respirators made of material sent up from G.H.Q. now being sent up with the bearer party nightly. No particulars extant with Sa-Femme yet this Division but Units receive many cases from other Divisions.	[A.D.M.S. 27th Division stamp]
5th May /15 EBBE FARM	Sick officers 2 other ranks 51. Wounded " 8 " 272. Casualties continue very heavy. 82nd Field Ambulance like one building to evacuees accommodation. 81st. Fd. Amb. opened in barnes Benedictine POPERINGHE — space for 300 cases. Great difficulty is now being experienced in getting patients from the trenches mostly on account of numbers – regiments bearers are played out. Bearer party 90 strong to Ward Rd. Fd. Amb. wounded – shrapnel left hand	J Marshall [?]

Army Form C. 2118.

WAR DIARY
or
INTELLIGENCE SUMMARY.
(Erase heading not required.)

Hour, Date, Place	Summary of Events and Information	Remarks and references to Appendices
6th May 15 EBBE FARM	Sick officers 2 otherranks 130 wounded " 3 " " 219 Notified D.m.s. as to shortage of Medical officers with Field Ambs. — we are now 9 M.O.s. 1 Quartermaster 100 Extra stretchers received from D.D.M.S. 5th Corps. Suggested that a Field Cooker be supplied to each Field Ambulance.	
7th May 15 " "	Sick officers 2 other ranks 98 wounded " 6 " " 228 Rather Field Ambulance ordered to leave POPERINGHE by shell fire School at BRANDHOEK opened as main Dressing Station and ECOLE— BIENFAISANCE East of YPRES is kept open as an Advanced Dressing Station. an Medical officer + 8 men remain there for D+ harm and are relieved daily from the Bearer Party.	J Murray Col

WAR DIARY or INTELLIGENCE SUMMARY

Army Form C. 2118.

(Erase heading not required.)

Hour, Date, Place	Summary of Events and Information	Remarks and references to Appendices
8th May '15 EBBE FARM	Sick Officers 15 other ranks 13 Wounded " 1 " 40 Lieut. J.A. Jones and D.M. Rowland arrive for duty.	
9th May '15	Sick officers 1 other rank 98. Wounded " 24 " 539. Very heavy casualties evacuated from cavalry Division of 5th Corps. 3 Vermorel Sprayers and up for cleaning gas out of trenches, they are despatched ready charged with solution and an extra petrol tin of solution is sent up with each sprayer. Lieut. R.G.L. McEntire and his Vermorels arrive as reinforcement for duty.	
10th May '15	Sick officers 17 other ranks 60 Wounded " 18 " — 539. Heavy shell fire continues on and around YPRES — and very heavy at Dressing Stations.	F.W. [signature]

Army Form C. 2118.

WAR DIARY
or
INTELLIGENCE SUMMARY.
(Erase heading not required.)

Instructions regarding War Diaries and Intelligence Summaries are contained in F.S. Regs., Part II. and the Staff Manual respectively. Title pages will be prepared in manuscript.

Hour, Date, Place	Summary of Events and Information	Remarks and references to Appendices
10th May '15 Continued	Lieut J.P. Mitchell wounded Medical officer to 4th K.R.R. Corps. Further supplies of material arrived for making 2000 mark.	
11th May '15. EBBE FARM.	Sick officers 1 other ranks 55 wounded — 18 — " — 47 — Lieut L.H. May annexis for duty. Posted to 4th KRRC as M.O. to 4 days. Then sent up with Bearer party for duty with 2nd Brigade R.B. gn.	
12th May '15.	Sick officers 4 other ranks 60 wounded — 13 — " — 310 Lieut M.L. Haywood Bond Id and officer to Bearer party wounded. Draft of 47 men arrived, including 6 n.c.os. for whom there are no vacancies. Wired D.G.M.S. reference shortage of Medical Officers.	J. McKenna Lieut-Col

Army Form C. 2118.

WAR DIARY
or
INTELLIGENCE SUMMARY.
(Erase heading not required.)

Hour, Date, Place	Summary of Events and Information	Remarks and references to Appendices
12th May '15 Continued —	25.00 Reinforcements sent up — making total to date 9950. Gave two Ambulances to Bearer Party Rank of Bearer Party 4 killed and 5 wounded in Cameroon dug-out.	(A.D.M.S. 27th DIVISION stamp)
13th May '15 EBBE FARM	Sick officers NIL other ranks 25 Wounded " 5 " " 181	
14th May '15 "	Sick officers 4 other ranks 17 Wounded " 4 " " 183 2nd Lieut. W.D. Anderson reported for duty and posted to 81st Field Amb. Reinforcements sent up for R.E. units. Lieut. E.A.P. Burch M.O. to 2nd R.I. was wounded and replaced by Lieut A.W. Venables.	
15th May '15 "	Sick officers NIL other ranks 47 Wounded " 1 " " 77 Lieut J.A. Fletcher and J.E. Pyken annexe J. Wakerwood into annexe	

Army Form C. 2118.

WAR DIARY
or
INTELLIGENCE SUMMARY.
(Erase heading not required.)

Instructions regarding War Diaries and Intelligence Summaries are contained in F.S. Regs., Part II. and the Staff Manual respectively. Title pages will be prepared in manuscript.

Hour, Date, Place	Summary of Events and Information	Remarks and references to Appendices
16th May 1915 EBBE FARM POPERINGHE	Sick officers 4 other ranks 46. Wounded " 2 " " " 77. And find that of 27th Division approximately one Casualties received tendency for each. Rising.	
17th May 1915 EBBE FARM.	Sick officers 1 other ranks 40. Wounded " - " " 45. " " - " " " 31. Commenced preparations for a Bathing Establishment in POPERINGHE by 50th Brigade relieved in front line by 3rd Cavalry Division came into rest at BUSSEBOOM. Capt. Williamson 6 days leave. Interviewed A.D.M.S. 3rd Cavalry Regt. vs taking over collecting area of 80th Bde.	[stamp: A.D.M.S. 27th DIVISION]
18th May '15	Sick officers NIL other ranks 19. Wounded " - " " " 31. Samples of water called for by D.M.S. in view of arsenic poisoning 81st Brigade being relieved by Cavalry tonight.	I Macwand Lt Col

Army Form C. 2118.

WAR DIARY
or
INTELLIGENCE SUMMARY.
(Erase heading not required.)

Instructions regarding War Diaries and Intelligence Summaries are contained in F.S. Regs., Part II. and the Staff Manual respectively. Title pages will be prepared in manuscript.

Hour, Date, Place	Summary of Events and Information	Remarks and references to Appendices
19th May 1915 EBBE FARM POPERINGHE	Sick officers 4 other ranks 5-8. Wounded — 2 " 3½. Forty Belt Tents received from Ordnance and distributed between Field Ambulances and Casualties and Bearer work have very light and we are now only responsible for half the usual length of time.	
20th May 1915 — " —	Sick officers 2 other ranks 44/3 Wounded — " — " — Several rainy. Whole air is being moved to each Unit for war if required and Peter Cradoc 3000 pairs are held in reserve. Sent A.E. Delgado reported during from Hospital and posted to 3rd Field Ambulance.	
21st May 1915 — " —	Sick officers 1 — other Ranks 5 6/13 Wounded " — " — " — Supply of respirators now in hand. Ordnance for same time as Field Dressings. Casualties lately very slight.	1 Wounded remained

(9 29 6) W 4141—463 100,000 9/14 HWV Forms/C. 2118;10

Army Form C. 2118.

WAR DIARY
or
INTELLIGENCE SUMMARY.
(Erase heading not required.)

Instructions regarding War Diaries and Intelligence Summaries are contained in F.S. Regs., Part II. and the Staff Manual respectively. Title pages will be prepared in manuscript.

Hour, Date, Place	Summary of Events and Information	Remarks and references to Appendices
22nd May 1915 EBBE FARM POPERINGHE	Sick officers 2 other ranks 46. Wounded " 1 " " 10 81st. Brigade came out to rest last night.	
23rd May '15	Sick officers Nil other ranks 44. Wounded " 2 " " 39. Gas was used by enemy in an attack last night. 27th Division now in rest. — 8 Regimental Medical Officers have been allowed short leave - two from 81st Field Ambulance A.D.M.S. also proceeded on leave on Medical [Survey?].	
24th May '15	Sick officers Nil other ranks 40. Wounded " " Nil " " 6 Gassed " " " " 21 27th Division keeping broken to eastern 80th Bde in advance - 81st. Bde in support. Medical Officers from Field Ambulances sent to all Units when R.M.O on leave. Bearer Party of half bat. — 1/2 to École Bienfaisance 1/2 to Casemate LILLE GATE. Gas attack early morning mostly by gas shells.	J Muirhead Lt Colonel R

Forms/C. 2118/12.

Army Form C. 2118.

WAR DIARY
or
INTELLIGENCE SUMMARY.
(Erase heading not required.)

Instructions regarding War Diaries and Intelligence Summaries are contained in F. S. Regs., Part II. and the Staff Manual respectively. Title pages will be prepared in manuscript.

Hour, Date, Place	Summary of Events and Information	Remarks and references to Appendices
24th. Continued. EBBE FARM.	3rd Field Ambulance report good results in Gas cases from treating with light inhalations of chloroform. Forms up to 14 days leave to Medical Officers. 7500 respirators repaired by Ordnance. Shortage of their article seems unnecessary. Heavy in fact – Divisional order re oxygen.	
25th May 15	Sick officers Nil other ranks 31 Wounded " 1 " " 141 Gassed " 2 " " 48 Warned to be ready to move to new area.	
26th May 15.	Sick officers Nil other ranks 42 Wounded " – " " 2 " – " " 77 3rd Fd Amb. marched to new area, to march by night via LOCRE Fd Field Ambulance detailed to move with them but ordered not to move at last moment. Very hot day. 80° more men fell out on march. Three Mob: Ambulances sent out to pick up. Casualties very heavy recently – two Bearers 3rd Field Ambulance slightly wounded.	I Mackenzie Lt Col R.A.M.C.

(9 29 6) W 4141—463 100,000 9/14 H W V Forms/C. 2118/10

Army Form C. 2118.

WAR DIARY
or
INTELLIGENCE SUMMARY.
(Erase heading not required.)

Hour, Date, Place	Summary of Events and Information	Remarks and references to Appendices
27th May '15 EBBE Farm.	Sick officers Nil. Other ranks 106. Wounded " 1 " " 1 80th Brigade returned to trenches – all wounded and sick removed by 12.15 a.m. Ordered 81st Fld Aml. to withdraw personnel from BRANDHOEK and advance D.D.M.S. 3rd Fld Amb Ambulance bivouacing to new area – to billet tonight at BAILLEUL. Lieut J.G. McGuire invalided to report to R.A.M.C. 28th Division for duty. Lieut B.L. Dunn evacuated sick.	
28th May '15	Sick officers 1. Other ranks 58. Wounded " – " " 13 81st Fld Ambulance now with 8th Brigade to new area. 3rd Field Amb. arrived at new site. ST JUDE – ARMENTIERES and took over Advanced Dressing Station from 18th F.A. and visited D.D.M.S. 3rd Corps and R.A.M.C. Cols. Division re taking over new area.	

J. Murray
Lt Col.

Army Form C. 2118.

WAR DIARY
or
INTELLIGENCE SUMMARY.
(Erase heading not required.)

Instructions regarding War Diaries and Intelligence Summaries are contained in F.S. Regs., Part II. and the Staff Manual respectively. Title pages will be prepared in manuscript.

Hour, Date, Place	Summary of Events and Information	Remarks and references to Appendices
29th May/15 EBBE FARM	Sick officers NIL other ranks 14 wounded — " — NIL SOUTH of STEEN WERCK 1st Field Ambulance arrived at Bellet. Took over the advanced Dressing Station from 1st Field Ambulance. No field Ambulance visits. All Field Ambulance and Field Ambulance submitted an improved type of respirator.	
30th May/15	Sick officers 1 other ranks 53 wounded — " — 7 Wrote 5th Cavalry Division re supply at Caëstre and the Coal supply depôt there.	
31st May/15 EBBS FARM POPERINGHE	Sick officers NIL other ranks 75 wounded — " — 5 80th Brigade Bearer & 3rd Field Ambulance march to LOCRE en route for new area. also Divisional Sanitary Section Workshop Section Division'l Headqrs. (including ADMS.) moved to New Area. Railway arrangements made to pick up stragglers en route by Ambulance Cars. Visited DDMS, 52 Corps, + D.Ms Ind Corps. also inspected Divisional Rest Station Key building Billets requested by 6th Division Eastward and by Commanding Unit of 27th Divn. too far a forwards came hither also convinced.	Movement Warrants adv. rd/as 27/6/vii

(9 29 6) W 4141—463 100,000 9/14 H W V App A to Forms/C.2118/10

G.S. 571.

Acting A.D.M.S.,
    27th Division.

    The Major General Commanding the Division wishes to congratulate all ranks of the R.A.M.C. (T) units under your command in this Division on the splendid and devoted work they have performed during the recent heavy fighting. He has watched with admiration the coolness and valour displayed however dangerous and delicate the task to be performed. The good result and the manner in which the combatant branches of the Division appreciate what has been done for their wounded must be a great satisfaction to you.

    The Major General heartily congratulates you and all ranks.

    These Territorial Units have proved that they can in difficulty and danger fully uphold the great traditions of their comrades in the Regular Service.

28th May, 1915.

                                          Lieut. Col., G.S.,
                                              27th Division.

27th D**ivision**

131/6023

June '15 — Items scored not copied 29/11/17

A.D.M.S. 27th Division

Vol VI

Army Form C. 2118.

WAR DIARY
or
INTELLIGENCE SUMMARY.
(Erase heading not required.)

Instructions regarding War Diaries and Intelligence Summaries are contained in F.S. Regs., Part II. and the Staff Manual respectively. Title pages will be prepared in manuscript.

Hour, Date, Place	Summary of Events and Information	Remarks and references to Appendices
1st. June /15 CROIX du BAC	Sick officers & other ranks 37 Wounded " " " 5 Three Medical officers, reinforcements, reported for duty & were posted two to 82nd F.A. and one to 8ist F.A. and Inspected all Dressing Stations, at Advanced Dressing Station, Regd Post. Recommendation sent and ample all round. Orders went for each Ambulance to submit a training programme. Saw Sanitary Section and arranged to continue with both Civil Military as organized by Late Division. Capt. E.L. Drake Cole, C.A.M.C. arrived to relieve Major E.B. Keenan as M.O. i/c P.P.C.L.I.	[27th DIVISION A.D.M.S. stamp]
2nd June /15	Sick officers 2 other ranks 25 Wounded " " " 11 Visited all ambulances. Major E.B. Keenan left to proceed to Hospital in London for duty in relief of officer in command of each section MO i/c B.R. train for all units in vicinity of Hon under	1 Movement 2 Morning was Stationary every night train 27th Div. Go.

Forms/C. 2118/10

WAR DIARY
or
INTELLIGENCE SUMMARY.
(Erase heading not required.)

Army Form C. 2118.

Instructions regarding War Diaries and Intelligence Summaries are contained in F.S. Regs., Part II. and the Staff Manual respectively. Title pages will be prepared in manuscript.

Hour, Date, Place	Summary of Events and Information	Remarks and references to Appendices
2nd June 1915	Sick officers 1 other ranks 55	
	Wounded " — " 1	
	Visited all Field Ambulances, D.D.M.S. 2nd Corps, visited 81st Field Ambulance and Divisional Rest Station at BAC ST MAUR. Divn orders re location of medical units	1
L.H. June 15	Sick officers 2 other ranks 48	
	Wounded " — " 10	
	Visited 81st, 82nd, 83rd Field Ambs. Cases of Cerebro Spinal Meningitis suspected in 19th Brigade. Lieut Col Kenny reported off leave. Rest Station for officers opened in ARMENTIERES. Met M.O. of de Brigade and also 9th Ambulances to draw unit sanitation Paraffin soap to be used weekly. Chloride of Lime to disinfect ditches and latrong farms. Lieut D Mathew evacuated sick	

J Mukanah
Lt Col M.D.

Army Form C. 2118.

WAR DIARY
or
INTELLIGENCE SUMMARY.
(Erase heading not required.)

Hour, Date, Place	Summary of Events and Information	Remarks and references to Appendices
5th June /15	Sick Officers 1 other ranks 3. Wounded " 1 " " 14. B.coe of 1st Durhams being 19th Brigade (5th Regular Rifles) compared. Three other cases suspected, sent in from same unit, received report at 3 pm. Apparently negative. Visited site and arranged isolation of seven contacts. Having the Advanced Dressing Stn of 80th Brigade to a be better placed for access at C.H. 6.8.2, and ordered closing of same A.D. Station in HOUPLINES in order to combine the two.	
6th June /15	Sick Officers 1 other ranks 19. Wounded " — " " 9. Seven cases of ENTERIC reported during past week, but no particular grouping or evidence of common source. There appears cases appear to be the spread of some water drunk during the recent fighting in the YPRES salient. where troops were obliged to possibly of keeping a supply of treated water.	

Army Form C. 2118.

WAR DIARY
or
INTELLIGENCE SUMMARY.
(Erase heading not required.)

Instructions regarding War Diaries and Intelligence Summaries are contained in F.S. Regs., Part II. and the Staff Manual respectively. Title pages will be prepared in manuscript.

Hour, Date, Place	Summary of Events and Information	Remarks and references to Appendices
7th June '15	Sick officers – other ranks 19 Wounded " 1 " " 51. Of the three suspected cases of Cerebro spinal Meningitis in 5th Cavalry Field Ambce, two are still in hospital little doubt that they are cases of Influenza. The positive bacteriological diagnosis of the first case however makes special care necessary.	
8th June '15	Sick officers – other ranks 30 Wounded " – " 12 Lieut Col. A.T. Martin and Capt. J.H. Keller arrived for duty, the former to command the 3rd Cav. Fd. Ambulance, the latter for duty – same unit. Arrangements made to attach Medical Officers of 3rd Amb. 13th Division to our Field Ambulances for instructions.	J Macowan J Cav Amb

WAR DIARY
or
INTELLIGENCE SUMMARY.
(Erase heading not required.)

Army Form C. 2118.

Hour, Date, Place	Summary of Events and Information	Remarks and references to Appendices
9th June /15	Sick officers — 1, other ranks 29. Wounded " — " " 1/3. Colonel E.G. BROWNE, R.A.M.C. arrived to take over as A.D.M.S. this Division. Thirel Flol. and Fme Field Ambulances & Divisional Rest Station detailed from empty One officer & further officers & thirty Lucy Amt to Reserve 6% and all having in Reserve and to act in advance to respective Brigades.	
10th June /15	Sick officers 1 other ranks 35. Wounded — " " 9. Inspection of Flot. Field Ambulance and Batn., BAC ST MAUR't Rest Station Arranged with R.A. the Pieces Officers J/c Brigades cleared work the Areas now allotted as Groups in order to include the units which have been split up and distributed in several Groups.	J. M. Irwin, Major

Army Form C. 2118.

WAR DIARY
or
INTELLIGENCE SUMMARY.
(Erase heading not required.)

Instructions regarding War Diaries and Intelligence Summaries are contained in F.S. Regs., Part II. and the Staff Manual respectively. Title pages will be prepared in manuscript.

Hour, Date, Place	Summary of Events and Information	Remarks and references to Appendices
11 Apr 1915	Sick officers 1 other ranks 26 wounded " " 10 R.A.P. No inspected 82nd & 83rd Field Ambulances and Sanitary Section. Capt. J Duncan to be detailed to undertake Sanitary Supervision of front area. He must not to be O.C. of Sanitary Section who remains O.C. of his Unit. Demonstration of Gas effect on Respirators at BAILLEUL. Report furnished to D.D.M.S. — Pad Respirators are not reliable and only a makeshift. Should be replaced by smoke helmet. The G.O.C. reported independently on enemy division lines.	
D.G. June 1st 1915	Sick officers — other ranks 23 wounded " " — " " 8. B.A.C. ST MAUR visited Baths and Laundry at field Ambulance 19th field Ambulance. Divisional order pursuance of Preparing of Field Ambulances	J Marcennell F.P. Lila Regt. C.

WAR DIARY
or
INTELLIGENCE SUMMARY.
(Erase heading not required.)

Army Form C. 2118.

Hour, Date, Place	Summary of Events and Information	Remarks and references to Appendices
13th June 1915.	Sick officers 1 Other ranks 13 Wounded " 1 " 6 Water Carts. - The water cart of this Division on general inspection found to be in a very bad condition nothing that the permits is a spark but on examination camp inspection of spark brought out stand. Camp inspection of spark door not provide for this - e.g. the inspector of the box in front are very light and she has itself to often need of a seat. & has to carry the extra weight of a man and perhaps horses. This may be irregular but it cannot be entirely prevented. Points work here - and connections of cylinders work loose - stake bars also. It is felt round the wash basin amounts to a tank on wheels, and it serves only for sterilization by chlorination. A.D.M.S visited 19th Field Ambulance, this unit is in a very high state of efficiency. C.O.s in M.s visited Dieneche - Remembered there is no anaphorectomy. D.O. in Medical Administration	[stamp: A.D.M.S. 27th DIVISION] J.W. Kemm II.

Army Form C. 2118.

WAR DIARY
or
INTELLIGENCE SUMMARY.
(Erase heading not required.)

Instructions regarding War Diaries and Intelligence Summaries are contained in F.S. Regs., Part II. and the Staff Manual respectively. Title pages will be prepared in manuscript.

Hour, Date, Place	Summary of Events and Information	Remarks and references to Appendices
14th June 1915.	Sick Officers 1 other ranks 193 Wounded " 1 " 192 Lieut J.W.B. Sherlock & H.Ors. to take D.R. Ms visited E.H.Ors. to take Major J. Barkery 83rd Field Ambulance evacuated 5 sick	(P.O. Wooley III Pampleler)
15th June '15	Sick officers 2 other ranks 16 Wounded " - " 14 San Luca Ambulance - Complaint Received from Officer re provisions from Home Reserve Units over due. Leap A.D.Ms not ordered for such the state of efficiency of the Units date of probable draft. &c Water.	IV.
16th June 1915.	Sick officers - other ranks 25. Wounded " - " 9. Inspected Camp of Divisional Ammu Column, also 96 & 98 Coy R.O. Train	J. Marchand Lt Colonel

WAR DIARY
or
INTELLIGENCE SUMMARY.
(Erase heading not required.)

Army Form C. 2118.

Hour, Date, Place	Summary of Events and Information	Remarks and references to Appendices
17th June 1915	Sick officers – other ranks 20 Wounded " 1 " 10 R.D.Mr visited 82nd Field Ambulance and informed the officers of their dissatisfaction on account of recent promotions. Also interviewed the senior N.C.O.'s of the unit at the same subject. Inspected Cyclist Coy Camp & 97th Coy A.S.C. – advised extra means of water Chlorination in first instance.	
18th June '15	Sick officers 2 other ranks 19 Wounded " " " 8 Visited Refuse Dump at PRES-DUHEM, seventy thousand tons of refuse here not burnt, merely kept away by late Divisions accepting but still gain daily more numerous. To be better to get rid of it. Major Wert find and Lengthsehal. Brig. Sir Free Sea Ambulance numerals J Muxworthy Accr. J McKenzie	

Form C. 2118/10

WAR DIARY
or
INTELLIGENCE SUMMARY.
(Erase heading not required.)

Army Form C. 2118.

Hour, Date, Place	Summary of Events and Information	Remarks and references to Appendices

19th June /16

Sick Officers – Other ranks. 25
Wounded " – " 3
1 Cpl. and 5 men arrive for
water duties with regimental units, conf.
from 28th Division.
Inspected trenches of Reserve
Regiment. Some lack of care
in latrine arrangement satisfactory.
Also billets of 2nd D.L.I. – what
reserve sanitation not well attended
to.

20th June /15

Sick Officers 1 other ranks 23
Wounded " – " 14
Lieut. J.Y. Dickson R amc S.C.
arrive for duty.
Visited billets of 4th KRRC in
Asylum. Sanitation not satisfactory,
especially latrines, huts by Rail
Division, encampment has few
about 400 men is being moved by 1000 to
further examination advised.
Saw Lawn Major R.E. question of retention of Arsenal. Collect G.S. T.M.

J. Mourand
Warand

Army Form C. 2118.

WAR DIARY
or
INTELLIGENCE SUMMARY.
(Erase heading not required.)

Instructions regarding War Diaries and Intelligence Summaries are contained in F.S. Regs., Part II. and the Staff Manual respectively. Title pages will be prepared in manuscript.

Hour, Date, Place	Summary of Events and Information	Remarks and references to Appendices
1st June 1915	Sick officers 1 other ranks 30 wounded " " " 7 Inspected billets of 82nd Brigade and all the Regimental Aid Posts, found in use by 2nd R. Scots Fus - 2 Coys in much happier state than that at K.R.R.C. but not sufficient fluid to admit of proper disinfection have advised "sump-pits" for use of water & of Creol solution on the top of contents.	
2nd June '15	Sick officers - other ranks 31 wounded " - " " 8 2nd Lt C.P. Kenny reported for departure for no 4 Stationary Hospital today. Visited Princess Louise Ambulance Divisional Orders on Sanitation	V attached

Army Form C. 2118.

WAR DIARY
or
INTELLIGENCE SUMMARY.
(Erase heading not required.)

Instructions regarding War Diaries and Intelligence Summaries are contained in F.S. Regs., Part II. and the Staff Manual respectively. Title pages will be prepared in manuscript.

Hour, Date, Place	Summary of Events and Information	Remarks and references to Appendices
23rd June 1915	Sick officers – Other ranks 19	
	Wounded " 1 " 6	
	Repeated attacks of 80th Brigade, too little appreciation of the importance of sanitary supervision is evident in many areas. Circulars letter to Medical Officers of Units on this question (Copy attached) → VI. VII.	
	Duncan Orders Instructions & water Supply	
24th June '15	Sick officers 3 other ranks 18	
	Wounded " 2 " 6	
	Sure Old Ambulances having faithful employment. Any R.D.M.S. not satisfied that care will be maintained when Captain B.G. Brown and Staff Serg Lehman are removed. Interviewed the O.C. and pointed out the importance of active control and attention to detail on the part of a Commanding Officer and saw	J Whitehead Sgt Mn Perm
	the measures to be	

WAR DIARY
or
INTELLIGENCE SUMMARY.
(Erase heading not required.)

Army Form C. 2118.

Hour, Date, Place	Summary of Events and Information	Remarks and references to Appendices
24th June (Continued)	be taken in case present officers do not rise to the situation. Inspected Bath of 2nd Brigade and saw the Brigadier, water boiling.	
25th June 1915.	Sick officers 1 other ranks 15. Wounded " 2 " " 8. Visited 19th Field Ambulance to water. Saw C.R.E. in reference to water survey of District. Shortage in greatly very apparent and expected in September.	VIII
26th June 1915.	Sick officers 3 other ranks 28 Wounded " 1 " " 4. Went round all Ambulances with a view to reducing number of division sick. No prospects of showing more than any few have as detained to such case are nearly dealt with by the units in billets. Dental case only to be sent to Dundril.	

J Moreland
L.T. Williams

Army Form C. 2118.

WAR DIARY
or
INTELLIGENCE SUMMARY.
(Erase heading not required.)

Instructions regarding War Diaries and Intelligence Summaries are contained in F.S. Regs., Part II. and the Staff Manual respectively. Title pages will be prepared in manuscript.

Hour, Date, Place	Summary of Events and Information	Remarks and references to Appendices
16th June 1915 (cont'd)	Dentist appears to be unnecessarily changing amalgam — also some eye cases sent for refractive error. New Guiness Accommodation in Divisional Rest Station to be renewed.	
27th July 1915	Sick Officers 1 Other ranks 27 wounded " 1 " 1 Inspected Billets of 2nd Gloucesters and Horse lines of 1st Royal Scots and 1st R. W. Regt. Never did regard in Sanitary routine. Letter to M.O. on subject. Inspected dugout and other smaller units. Sick Officers — Other ranks 14 wounded " — " 5 Inspected Billets of 9th Royal Scots and 1st Royal Scots. Latter not bad. Visited Red Sea Ambulance — carry out improvements.	J. Wakeman Lt Col

28th July 1915
Continued

Stretchers of underfeeds called, certainly good, many our troops and affects the dislike of freeh. Arrangements made for supplements blood examination of suspected cases. Bad case of tourniquet left on too long by Col Sweir Ambulance (no neglect died - weak line of treatment)

29th July 1915

Sick officers - Attenuated 20
Wounded   "   "   11
Branch for water closed and Chlorinator distributed to small units not having a water cart.

Steen Gs. Report sent to Q.
Factory occupied by 81st Tweed Ambulance is required to carry on by anyone.

Inspected several site for Breakdown Ambulance.

[signature] [signature]

Army Form C. 2118.

WAR DIARY
or
INTELLIGENCE SUMMARY.
(Erase heading not required.)

Instructions regarding War Diaries and Intelligence Summaries are contained in F. S. Regs., Part II. and the Staff Manual respectively. Title pages will be prepared in manuscript.

Hour, Date, Place	Summary of Events and Information	Remarks and references to Appendices
30th June 1915. CROIX DU BAC.	Sick officers NIL Other Ranks 34. Wounded " " " 1 - 12. Medical Officers and Ambulance detailed to attend at Bombing School where several accident have already occurred. Sanitary Report for month of June despatches, copy attached IX. Sgt. H. Rush R.A.M.C. once proceeded on leave. Field Ambulances. 5 patients have several Sick in Medical Ward of 822.	[stamp: A.D.M.S. 27th DIVISION] [signature]

[signature] E.G. Browne Colonel A.M.S. A.D.M.S. 27th Division

DIVISIONAL ROUTINE ORDERS No.4.

by

MAJOR GENERAL T.D'O. SNOW, C.B. Commanding 27th. Division.

2nd. June 1915.

24. LOCATION OF FIELD AMBULANCES.
Order No. 23 of Divisional Routine Orders No.3 of 2nd June is cancelled and the following substituted:-

80th. Brigade - 83rd. Field Ambulance ECOLE PROFESSIONNELLE Sq. B 30 b-d.
Advanced Dressing Station Sq. I 7 b 8.9

81st. Brigade.- 81st. Field Ambulance at ERQUINGHEM Sq. H 3 d 9.2
Advanced Dressing Station Sq. I 1 d 6.4

82nd. Brigade - 82nd Field Ambulance at Institute St. JUDE Sq. B 30 d 9.8.
Advanced Dressing Stations at Sq. C 21 b 4.2 and C 13 b 8.2.

19th. Brigade. 19th. Field Ambulance at ERQUINGHEM near the church.
Advanced Dressing Station Sq. H 24 b 1.9.

25. SPIES.
Attention is drawn to pages 32 - 35 "SPIES" of " Extracts from General Routine Orders issued to the British Army in the Field" of 1st March 1915, the gist of which should again be made known to all ranks.
Any Officer N.C.O. or man having good reason to suspect the presence of a spy, particularly in uniform, or receiving such information from local inhabitants is to report the matter immediately to the A.P.M. 27th. Division, 66 RUEde DUNKERQUE in ARMENTIERES and to his Commanding Officer who will forward the evidence in writing as soon as possible to the A.P.M.
Commanding Officers of units will, at the same time, warn Divisional Headquarters, repeating to Infantry Brigades, Divisional Yeomanry and Cyclists in order that the Guards over the River LYS may be warned as soon as possible.
Any suspicious character whether in uniform or not, asking questions as to location or movements of troops etc., is to be arrested immediately and taken to the nearest guard or to the A.P.M.

26. SUPPLIES.
Refilling of supply wagons of Artillery Units will in future be carried out by Brigades and not by Batteries.

27. GREEN FORAGE.
The cost of green forage is approximately 40 to 50 francs per 900 square metres.

28. INDENTS.
Indents for Ordnance Stores except in cases of emergency will be signed by the Officer Commanding the Unit or in his absence by the next senior officer: non-compliance with this order will only cause delay.

29. DIVISIONAL ROUTINE ORDERS.
Notices for publication in current day's issue of Divisional Routine Orders must be in this office by 1 p.m.

P.T.O.

30 PURCHASE OF SUPPLIES.
The following instructions will, in future, be strictly complied with:-
(1) A separate return as per pro-forma issued herewith, will be rendered in Triplicate to Divisional Headquarters weekly of all supplies purchased. This return will be compiled up to and including Thursday of each week, and will be rendered to Divisional Headquarters by noon Friday. Nil returns to be rendered.
(2) Units are only entitled to purchase :-
   (a) Vegetables (½ lb. per man per day)
       1 kilo - 5 rations.
   (b) Fuel, Wood or Coal (3 lbs wood or 1½ lbs coal)
       per man per day.
   (c) Forage to supplement present hay ration.
       (2 lbs. extra for horses L.D.)
        5 lbs. :   :   :   H.D.)
(3) The vegetable ration is based on that of potatoes, and, if Units purchase more expensive vegetables, the monetary value of potatoes must not be exceeded, and the proportion of weight will in consequence be reduced.
(4) The monetary value of fodder purchased to supplement hay must not exceed that of local cost of hay.
(5) Units must purchase on a weekly basis - Overdrawals will not be permitted, and underdrawals will be forfeited.
(6) Coal may not be purchased without reference to Supply Officer of "formation".
(7) No articles other than those stated in (3) may be purchased nor can they be taken on charge by Supply Officers. Field Ambulances however, may make purchases of extras such as milk, flour etc., for patients.
(8) The current rates of local prices will be published from time to time, and should these be exceeded when making purchases, an explanation will be given.
(9) Linseed and Bran may not be purchased to supplement the Hay Ration. A limited quantity of both these commodities for sick horses, can be obtained from Railhead on Veterinary Officer's certificate accompanying demand.
(10) The usual weekly return of other articles purchasedX will be rendered as heretofore but on a separate paper.

X or requisitioned

31. POSTAL ARRANGEMENTS.
Deliveries. Post Orderlies from all Units except those mentioned below must be at the Army Post Office, PLACE de REPUBLIC, ARMENTIERES, at 11-30 a.m. with conveyances to draw the Mails.
The Orderlies from the undermentioned Units must attend at the Divisional Headquarters Field Post Office, at 11-15 a.m. for the same purpose:-
   Divisional Headquarters (including R.A.)
   "A" Squadron Surrey Yeomanry.
   Wessex Signal Company.
   27th. Divisional Cyclist Company.
   27th. Field Ambulance Workshops.
   16th. Mobile Veterinary Section.

The Bags for the 27th. Divisional Supply Column will be drawn at Railhead at 11 a.m. and the bags for the 27th Divisional Ammunition Park will be drawn at the CAESTRE Railhead A.P.O.
Postings. The orderlies must take in overnight to the A.P.O's where they draw their mails as much correspondence and as many parcels as possible.

Official letters for delivery the same day at G.H.Q., 2nd. Army Hd.Qrs. and Corps Headquarters throughout the Second Army, should be posted at the A.P.O., PLACE de REPUBLIC, ARMENTIERES or Divisional Troops Post Office not later than 9 a.m.

Postings for England and down country which cannot be brought in earlier may be posted at the F.P.Os. PLACE de REPUBLIC ARMENTIERES up to 11-30 am. and at Divisional Troops Post Office up to 11-45 a.m. to connect with the outgoing afternoon mail from Railhead but every effort should be made to include as much as possible in the overnight despatch.

H.J. EVERETT COLONEL.

A.A. & Q.M.G. 27th. Division.

NOTICE.

FOUND. Dun coloured gelding - aged 7 years - No. 36 on off hind - Star Blaze.
Application for the animal should be made to O.C. Warwick Heavy Battery R.G.A.

DIVISIONAL ROUTINE ORDERS - No.13.

by

MAJOR GENERAL T.D'O.SNOW, C.B., Commanding 27th. Division.

13th. June 1915.

83. LEAVE.
(a) Trains -
Under instructions from R.T.O., Railhead, N.C.O's and men proceeding to England on furlough should report at the station STEENWERCK by 4-10 p.m. in order to depart by the 5-11 p.m. train.
There is no accomodation on the French train at 7-19 p.m. for the numbers allowed.
(b) Warrants.
Neither the Base Stationery Office nor 3rd.Corps are able to supply Books of Warrants. Manuscript Warrants in the following form are all that is necessary :-

RAILWAY WARRANT

The Directors of the S.E. and Chatham Railway Company are hereby requested to provide conveyance from Boulogne Station to _____ (and return), for the undermentioned party, the Fare to be defrayed by the War Office
(Class of ticket to be stated)

Date.   Signature
                                                   Rank and Unit.

84. DRESS.
Attention is drawn to General Routine Order 55 in which the wearing of flowers and other unsoldierly trinkets in the cap is forbidden.

85. LOCATION OF FIELD AMBULANCES.
Reference Divisional Order No.24 dated 3rd.instant, the Advanced Dressing Station of 80th.Brigade (83rd.Field Ambulance) has now moved to square C 26 b 9.2.

86. MEDICAL ADMINISTRATION.
Field Ambulances are attached to Brigades as follows :-
19th. to 19th. Infantry Brigade.

81st. to 81st. Infantry Brigade.

82nd. to 82nd Infantry Brigade.

83rd. to 80th. Infantry Brigade.

In order to decentralize the Medical and Sanitary work of the Division, Officers Commanding Field Ambulances will in all local matters affecting health and sanitation, advise Brigade Commanders direct, forwarding to A.D.M.S. copies of any recommendations they make.

87. LEAVE.
Officers and other ranks proceeding on leave of absence will invariably take with them, for production when demanded, the written authority granting such leave..
(G.R.O.911).

P. T. O.

88. EFFECTS OF DECEASED SOLDIERS.
With reference to General Routine Order No.423 dated 12th. December, 1914, the following additional instructions are published :-
In the case of men who are known to have died of an infectious disease, all effects sent to the D.A.G. Base, must be thoroughly disinfected and a certificate enclosed (in the same parcel with the effects) stating that this has been done.
No articles of personal clothing are in any case to be sent with the effects.
(G.R.O. 913).

89. BURIAL OF DEAD HORSES.
Complaints having been received from inhabitants that horses have been buried with an insufficient covering of earth, it is notified for information that this covering should be as deep as possible, and in no case less than four feet in depth. If possible, lime should be freely sprinkled on the carcass.
(G.R.O.914).

90. EQUIPMENT - DIVISIONAL MOUNTED TROOPS.
Approval is given for the issue of one "Horrock's Portable Water Clarifier" to Divisional Mounted Troops, to be carried on existing transport.
Indents should be sent to Ordnance Officers concerned, and issue will be made as supplies become available.
(G.R.O. 916).

91. EYE FRINGES.
Approval is given for the issue of eye fringes on a scale of one per animal.
Indents should be sent to Ordnance Officers concerned, and issue will be made as supplies become available.
(G.R.O.917).

92. INEFFECTIVE HORSES.
General Routine Order No.537 is cancelled and the following substituted :-
Ineffective horses which are not veterinary cases, may be evacuated, by the authority of Corps Commanders. Descriptive rolls giving reasons for recommending evacuation will be forwarded in the first place to the D.D.R. of the Army or D.A.D.R. of the Cavalry Corps concerned, who will enter his remarks on the roll for information of Corps Commander.
Horses evacuated under this order will be handed over to Mobile Veterinary Sections.
(G.R.O. 918).

93. PROMOTIONS - WARRANT AND NON-COMMISSIONED OFFICERS.
The attention of all concerned is directed to General Routine Order No.906, dated 10th. June, 1915, on the subject of Promotions of Warrant and Non-Commissioned Officers. All previous General Routine Orders on this subject are cancelled.

E.H. COLLEN, MAJOR.

for A.A. & Q.M.G. 27th. Division

NOTICE.

FOUND. In "A" Battery, 53rd. Brigade R.F.A. Wagon Lines (H 8 a 5.4.) near ERQUINGHEM on the morning of 11th.June, Bay Mare L.D. white stocking near hind, white blazes. On the off Fore letter T, on near fore number 84. SLC 7 is stamped on the head collar.

DIVISIONAL ROUTINE ORDERS. No. 14.

by

MAJOR GENERAL T. D'O. SNOW, C.B., Commanding 27th. Division.

15th. June 1915.

94. **WATER FOR ANALYSIS.**
Samples of water for analysis may now be sent to 83rd Field Ambulance ECOLE PROFESSIONELLE.
Any new supplies and any others not known to be good should be submitted by units. Special care must be taken to send samples in clean bottles with clean corks, and the bottles to be used should previously be well rinsed out with water from the same supply from which the sample is to be taken.

95. **DISINFECTANTS.**
There have recently been several complaints of insufficient supply of cresol. It is possible that this disinfectant is being used in too great quantities, or too strong. The proper strength of the solution for buckets and for general use is 1 in 160 or 4 table-spoonsful to 1 gallon. Buckets should be filled to a depth of about 3 inches with the above solution. Sides of buckets should be kept clean and occasionally rubbed over with a strong solution of cresol.

96. **LOOPHOLE PLATES & GERMAN BULLETS.**
Any bullet or part of a bullet, which is known to have pierced a loophole plate and which can be recovered should be sent to C.E. 3rd. Corps. The plate pierced should be examined and any record of any special marking (or manufacturers name) on the plate, together with the probable range at which the bullet was fired, should be forwarded at the same time.

97. **HORSES FOR CASTING.**
With reference to 2nd Army Routine Order No.97, dated 22nd May 1915, it is notified for the information of all concerned that horses which it is proposed to cast for reasons other than veterinary, will be sent to the Headquarter Company of the 27th.Divisional Train for inspection by the D.D. of R., 2nd Army.
This inspection will be held on the second Wednesday in each month at 3 p.m.
Officers Commanding Units will forward to this Office, through the usual channels, at least 3 clear days prior to the inspection, the casting roll referred to in Divisional Routine Order No.92 dated 13th. instant.

98. **COURTS MARTIAL-EVIDENCE AS TO CHARACTER OF ACCUSED.**
This should always be given and recorded on the proceedings.
A complete copy of Army Form B.296 (statement as to character, etc., of the accused) need not be attached, but the Court should take and record such evidence as to character as is available. Usually the Field Conduct Sheet is produced by the prosecutor. A copy may be attached, otherwise extracts will be recorded by the Court, e.g., "two entries for drunkenness, one for absence from the trenches".
It is not competent for the Court to take verbal evidence of the accused being a BAD character. The badness of his character must be proved by former convictions and entries in the Field Conduct Sheet, and not by the expression of any opinion to that effect by witnesses, although such opinion is admissible as evidence of GOOD character.
(A.R.O.116).

P.T.O.

99. ARRIVALS AND DEPARTURES
Calais now being a Base Port, the attention of Officers and other ranks leaving or returning to France by that port is drawn to the necessity of reporting themselves to the Base Commandant in accordance with General Routine Order No.329 dated 16th, November 1914,(Extracts from General Routine Orders,1st March, 1915 page 7.).
(A.R.O.118).

100. DISCIPLINE.
Officers and men who may have discarded their jackets,due to heat or any other cause, must invariably wear their equipment including smoke helmet and respirator, except when in CLOSE proximity to their billets or bivouacs.
(A.R.O.120-.)

101. LETTERS SENT THROUGH THE SIGNAL SERVICE.
The attention of all concerned is drawn to General Routine Order No. 117 dated 12th. June. 1915 regarding the despatch of letters through the Signal Service.

102. PASSES.
The blue card pass is sufficient for journeys by motor car or bicycle to G.H.Q. via Cassel.
Boulogne is French Area and in this case a pink pass is required. Such passes will be issued by the A.P.M. on application.

103. COURTS MARTIAL.
Officers Commanding Units are reminded that Court Martial Prisoners, will be kept with their unit until instructions are received from the A.P.M. as to their disposal.

104. ABSENTEES.
All absentees will be reported to the A.P.M. giving description.

E.H. COLLEN, Major,

for A.A. & Q.M.G. 27th. Division.

DIVISIONAL ROUTINE ORDERS No. 15.

by

MAJOR GENERAL T.D'O. SNOW, C.B., Commanding 27th. Division.

15th. June 1915.

105. **FIELD GENERAL COURT MARTIAL.**
The detail of Officers as mentioned below will assemble at Headquarters Divisional Yeomanry Squadron, (G 11 a 2.2) at 10 a.m. on Thursday 17th. June 1915, for the purpose of trying, by Field General Court Martial, the undermentioned and such other persons as may be brought before them ;-
   No.5743, Pte J.Haughey, 27th. Divisional Cyclist Company,
       Army Cyclist Corps.

PRESIDENT.
Major C.A. Calvert, Surrey Yeomanry.
MEMBERS.
A Captain, A.S.C. to be detailed by O.C.27th. Divisional Train.
A Lieutenant to be detailed by O.C. 27th. Divisional Cyclist Co.
                                (at least one years service).

The accused will be warned and all witnesses duly required to attend.
The proceedings will be forwarded to this Office.

106. **STRENGTH.**
(1) Brigadier General the Hon.F.Gordon, C.B., D.S.O. having been appointed to command a Division of the New Armies, relinquished yesterday the command of the 19th. Infantry Brigade.
(2) Lieut Colonel P.R.Robertson, C.M.G., 1st Cameronians has been appointed to command the 19th. Infantry Brigade from 14th. June 1915, with the Temporary rank of Brigadier General.
(3) Captain F.T.Cox, A.S.C., assumes the duty of Senior Supply Officer, 27th. Division, vice Major G.M.Young, appointed D.A.Q.M.G. 25th. Division.

107. **SURPLUS RATIONS.**
Reference Divisional Routine Order No.17 (b) dated June 1st. all units in possession of surplus rations will immediately take steps to underdraw rations to the extent of the surpluses shewn on returns. The process will be gradually effected by indenting for not more than 10% less each day.

108. **ANTI-GAS APPARATUS.**
After a gas attack all smoke helmets and respirators which have been subjected to the gas are to be returned at once to the 83rd. Field Ambulance, Ecole Professionnelle where they will be redipped under the orders of A.D.M.S. and subsequently re-issued.

109. **WATER.**
It has been brought to notice that troops are drinking water from pumps, stand pipes and other sources, the purity of which is questionable.
It should be impressed on all concerned that only water from water-carts, that has been properly treated should be used for drinking purposes by the troops. It is the duty of Medical Officers i/c units, Company Officers, Platoon Commanders and all N.C.O's to see that this order is rigidly enforced.

110. **RESPIRATORS.**
Each man not in possession of a smoke helmet will carry two respirators.

P. T. O.

111. HONOURS AND REWARDS.
Attention is drawn to Circular Memorandum No. 1611, "Honours and Rewards" issued with Divisional Routine Orders this day, to all concerned.

H.J. EVERETT   COLONEL.

A.A. AND Q.M.G. 27th. Division.

NOTICE.

LOST. Burberry Coat with fleece lining.
Taken from end of communication trench, between 1st and 2nd line of support trenches behind Chard's Farm about 10 p.m. 11-6-1915.
Finder please communicate with Captain Long "B" Company 2nd. Cameron Highlanders.

DIVISIONAL ROUTINE ORDERS No.22

by

MAJOR GENERAL T.D'O SNOW, C.B., Commanding 27th Division.

22nd June 1915.

142. CAPTURED TROPHIES, ARMS ETC.

G.R.O. No. 549 is republished for information and compliance.

"Attention is called to Field Service Regulations Part II, "Section 118-2. All ranks are reminded that captured trophies "guns arms, ammunition, equipment, vehicles, and other stores "are the property of the Government and, if not ordered to be "destroyed, must be handed over to the nearest Ordnance or "Transport Officer.
"The Custom Officials in England will seize any such "articles whether sent or taken over by individual officers "and soldiers".

143. SANITATION. (a). <u>Fly Prevention.</u> The practice of throwing half empty beef tins and other scraps of food over the front parapet is forbidden. This rule should be rigidly enforced.

A continuous effort to keep down the fly nuisance should be made by everyone for the next two months.

The house fly breeds mostly in horse dung and is attracted by sweet and greasy debris of food. All dung must therefore be burned and no food scraps be left lying about.

The blue bottle breeds mostly in filth and in decayed carcases and ground near them, so all meat tins, bones, carcases etc. which cannot be burned should buried as deeply as possible and never less than 1 foot below the surface.

Cresol solution 1.160 sprayed or sprinkled about will materially help to keep flies away.

All meat, food, bread, jam, etc., should be kept covered over or in safes made out of wooden frames and gauze sides.

(b).<u>LATRINES.</u> The use of earth to cover the faeces is a practice essential in all trench latrines (latrines dug in the ground, whether shallow or deep) and should be strictly enforced.

When, however, buckets are in use, dry earth should not be used, but a sufficient quantity of cresol solution placed in the buckets to keep their contents covered.

144. BATHS. Attention is called to instructions previously issued. Parties proceeding to the baths will invariably be armed.

H.J. EVERETT COLONEL,

A.A. and Q.M.G. 27th Division.

DIVISIONAL ROUTINE ORDERS, No. 23,

by

MAJOR GENERAL T. D'O. SNOW, C.B., Commanding 27th Division.

23rd June 1915.

145. **ARMOURERS SHOP.** A Divisional Armourers Shop has been established at ERQUINGHEM.

With the exception of the 19th Infantry Brigade, who have their own shop, and the Infantry Battalions of the 80th Infantry Brigade, all units in the Division which require arms, machine guns or bicycles repaired should take them to this shop.

No indents for bicycles to replace unserviceable will be accepted by the D.A.D.O.S. from any unit in the Division, unless the bicycle has been first inspected and a certificate obtained from the shop that it is beyond repair.

Receipts will be given for all articles handed into the shop.

146. **BURIALS.** With reference to Circular Memorandum No. 1575 dated 12th instant, permission is granted for 5th Scottish Rifles to use L'ARMEE cemetery.

147. **SMOKE HELMETS.** Attention is drawn to Divisional Routine Order No. 52 of 7th instant, paragraph (d).

148. **INOCULATION.** The monthly inoculation return will be rendered to A.D.M.S. on the 26th instant by all units, as per pro forma:-

UNIT.	Strength		Inoculated.	
	Offrs.	O. Ranks.	Offrs.	O. Ranks.

149. **WATER.** The pump and well water in this area appears to require more Chloride of Lime to effect complete chlorination than normal clear water. The fill of the small measure contained in each tin will, for the present, be taken as the amount necessary to chlorinate one water cart. Tests will be made to find out the exact quantity required and further instructions will be issued in due course.

Great care should be taken that the chloride of lime is thoroughly broken up and dissolved before being put into the cart. Medical Officers i/c Units will supervise the water duty orderlies in order to ensure that this is done.

150. **FIELD GENERAL COURT MARTIAL.** The detail of Officers as mentioned below will assemble at Headquarters 27th Divisional Column STEENWERCK, at 10 a.m. Friday 25th June, 1915, for the purpose of trying by Field General Court Martial, the undermentioned and such other persons as may be brought before them.

No. M/2. 019057 Mech. Staff Sergt. T. Ward, A.S.C., 27th Divisional Supply Column.

President/

PRESIDENT.

Lieut. Colonel A.T. Liddell, A.S.C., Commanding
27th Divisional Train.

MEMBERS.

A Captain, 27th Divisional Ammunition Column.
A Subaltern, 27th Divisional Cyclist Company.
(At least one year's service).

The accused will be warned and all witnesses duly required to attend.

The proceedings will be forwarded to this Office.

H.J. EVERETT COLONEL,
A.A. and Q.M.G, 27th Division.

DIVISIONAL ROUTINE ORDERS No. 24

BY

MAJOR GENERAL T.D'O. SNOW, C.B., Commanding 27th Division.

24th June 1915.

151. WATER TESTING.
It is notified for general information that a chemical case for the rapid testing of metallic poisons in water is being issued, 1 to each Medical Officer i/c of a regiment, 3 to each Field Ambulance (1 per Section), and one to each Divisional Sanitary Section.

Instructions for use are pasted inside the case.

All water supplies likely to have been poisoned should be tested before use by the troops, and if found to contain poison, steps should be taken to ensure that the use of the water is prohibited and the water supply distinctly marked "POISONED".

A sample of the water should be sent immediately to the 83rd Field Ambulance, and another sample to the D.M.S. 2nd Army direct.

This apparatus is an Army Service Corps supply, and should therefore be obtained from the Officer Commanding, Base Supply Stores, through Formation Supply Officers.

152. SMOKE HELMETS.
A diagram is issued with orders, illustrating the correct method of folding smoke helmets. The advantage of this method is that the eyepiece can be inspected without taking the helmet out of its bag, and the eyepiece itself being in the centre of the folds and quite flat, is much less liable to injury. The helmet should never be taken out of its bag except for use.

Company Officers will take immediate steps to introduce this method of folding, and will, after the 26th instant be held personally responsible should helmets carried by men under their command be found to be improperly folded.

At present the wastage in smoke helmets is excessive and it must cease. The rate of wastage is such, that if it continued, it will take weeks to build up a reserve.

Attention is called to the memorandum issued with orders on the 11th instant. The order as regards the detailed weekly inspection of smoke helmets and respirators on Saturdays does not appear to have been carried out in some cases.

153. INTERPRETERS.
The following transfers have been authorised:-
Monsieur GOVARE, Officer Interpreter 3rd Class,
 from H.Q. 80th Infantry Bde. to H.Q. 27th Divn.

Monsieur KERGALL, Interpreter Stagiaire, from
 H.Q. 81st Infantry Bde. to H.Q. 80th Infy. Bde.

154. DIVINE SERVICE.   Church of England.
(1). Infantry Brigades.
Brigade Chaplains will arrange with Commanding Officers for Parade Services, where possible, for units of their Brigade and for certain Divisional Units billeted in their area, and will communicate to all concerned the times and places of such parade Services.

(2). Remainder of Divisional Troops.

    7.30 a.m. Holy Communion.
                Place 27th Divisional Dressing
                Station. Divisional Headquarters.

    9.30 a.m. Parade Service.
                Place H.Q. 27th Divnl. Ammn. Col.
                                (H 1 b 1.9)
                Troops - Divnl. Ammn. Col. only.

    10.30 a.m. Parade Service.
                Place - Billet of 39th Battery
                            (E 27 d 6.9)
                Troops - All units billeted North
                of River LYS but East of a N. and S
                line through JESUS Farm (B 26 d)

    11.30 a.m. Parade Service
                Place Divisional Baths, (H 5 a).
                Troops - all units billeted SOUTH
                of River LYS but East of a N. & S.
                line through ERQUINGHEM Bridge.

    12. Noon. Holy Communion.

    2.30 p.m. Parade Service.
                Place "A" Battery 53rd F.A. Bde
                Farm (H 8 b).
                Troops - all Units billeted SOUTH
                of River LYS but WEST of a N & S
                line through ERQUINGHEM Bridge.

    4.30 p.m. Parade Service.
                Place - 27th Divnl. Headquarters in
                Field opposite 27th Divisional
                Dressing Station.
                Troops - All units except 27th Divnl
                Ammunition Column billeted NORTH of
                River LYS but WEST of a N. and S.
                line through JESUS Farm (B 26 d).

(3). The above are Parade Services and all ranks except those on duty or for other legitimate reasons excused by Commanding Officers will attend.

                                H.J. EVERETT COLONEL,

          A.A. and Q.M.G. 27th Division.

27th Division

121/6439

A.D.M.S. 27th Division

Vol III

From 1st to 31st July 1915.

13/6439

Summarised but not copied
Dec. 1922.

A.D.M.S. 27th Div. July 7?

App. 3 - has been
detached & filed
under "Gas" 6

Army Form C. 2118.

WAR DIARY
or
INTELLIGENCE SUMMARY.
(Erase heading not required.)

Instructions regarding War Diaries and Intelligence Summaries are contained in F.S. Regs., Part II. and the Staff Manual respectively. Title pages will be prepared in manuscript.

Hour, Date, Place	Summary of Events and Information	Remarks and references to Appendices
1st July 1915 — CROIX DU BAC.	Sick officers Nil Other Ranks 39 Wounded " 1 " " 15 Visit of Lieut-Col. (Roperny) Chappas from Tenth Headquarters to see our Medical arrangements at the front. Saw Tweeter Aid Post and Advanced Dressing Station of 19th Field Ambulance. Was impressed by number of our incinerators. D.M.L. 2nd Army called. Divisional Order published re use of Anti paraffin.	[27th Division A.D.M.S. stamp] J. Murray Lt. Col. A.D.M.S.
2nd July '15	Sick officers Nil Other ranks 16 Wounded " Nil " " 5 Instructions issued to O's C. Fd Amb. re examination of blood for cases suspected Malaria. Sanitary Officer 2nd Army asked to cause re steps to be taken to provide water supplies. Well water in this country is all suspect, founded no pollution direct to well occurs, heat than is almost universal. Sgd Lieut R.H. Bauer RAMC 27 Divnl 83rd Field Ambulance from Sick Leave.	DW

Army Form C. 2118.

WAR DIARY
or
INTELLIGENCE SUMMARY.
(Erase heading not required.)

Instructions regarding War Diaries and Intelligence Summaries are contained in F.S. Regs., Part II. and the Staff Manual respectively. Title pages will be prepared in manuscript.

Hour, Date, Place	Summary of Events and Information	Remarks and references to Appendices
3rd July 1915 CROIX du BAC	Sick officers 1 other ranks 31. Wounded — 4 — 5. A.D.M.S. visited 80th & 81st Field and Rest Stations, 82nd & 83rd Field Ambce & Sanitary Section. Medical Carparks for Regiment are to be drawn in future from R Medical Officers known Field Ambulances — who will replenish their stock once a week from supplies.	[signature]
4th July 1915	Sick officers 1 other ranks 20. Wounded — Nil — Nil — 6. Searched for new water supplies with Sanitary officer 2nd Army. They are several deep wells in the area attached to Brewries which give prospect of large and good supply. Also if secured, there are canteens kept — e.g. H 17 d — shed 26 — which could be rendered potable by cleaning of same and Chlorination.	[signature]

Army Form C. 2118.

WAR DIARY
or
INTELLIGENCE SUMMARY.
(Erase heading not required.)

Hour, Date, Place	Summary of Events and Information	Remarks and references to Appendices
5th July 1915 CROIX du BAC	Sick officers 1 other ranks 21 wounded — nil " " 5 Demonstration of method of stamping Smoke Helmets by Lieut Barkly, R.E. Army Expert. The object being to keep the fabric supple and the windows from cracking. Spraying the helmets fully opened out is recommended. It appears that to keep a quick back of feel or bandage blanket folded in opposite the window which can be taken out and damped in solution. beneficially in a much simpler and equally effective method. Inspected transports of 81st & 82nd Field Ambulance. Very great improvement especially in the former.	JMcC
6th July 1915	Sick officers — other ranks 33 wounded — nil " 10 R.D.Mr inspected Field Lila Ambulance Room Dressing Station & personnel — very satisfactory. Capt. E.G. Browne D.S.O. & Major F.J. Brian reporting their respective units. Lieut. M. Tabrin ordered to proceed to Indian for duty. Divisional order in water supply.	JMcC

Army Form C. 2118.

WAR DIARY
or
INTELLIGENCE SUMMARY.
(Erase heading not required.)

Hour, Date, Place	Summary of Events and Information	Remarks and references to Appendices
7th July 1915. CROIX du BAC.	Sick officers NIL other ranks 14 Wounded " NIL " 7 A number of reinforcements recently arrived have been found unfit for service at the front and returned to the Base. A draft of ten sent down today.	[stamp: A.D.M.S. 27th DIVISION] JM
8th July '15.	Sick officers 3 other ranks 77. Wounded " 1 other rank 4. Lt. Lent. J.F. Buckeridge R.A.M.S. proceeded on leave. Capt M.J. Williamson R.A.M.C. posted as A.D.M.S. temporarily vice Lieut Colonel proceeded to Indian Corps.	JM
9th July '15.	Sick officers NIL other ranks 31 Wounded " 2 " 10 A.D.M.S. inspected Rest Station at BAC ST MAUR and various parts of sanitary interest in ARMENTIÈRES. The latter included the dumping ground, which has been by arrangement of R.E. now altered by him to the abattoir, in regard to which a letter was sent to Town Major pointing out the existence of fly-ridden heaps of manure & acetic compounds Blood.	JM

Army Form C. 2118.

WAR DIARY
or
INTELLIGENCE SUMMARY.
(Erase heading not required.)

Hour, Date, Place	Summary of Events and Information	Remarks and references to Appendices
9th July Continued	Also inspected the Inn Charles Lyons. Visit of Inspector of M.S. Vehicles. Captain G Dundas Rawe J.D. from DIEPPE as Sanitary Inspector.	
10th July 1915. CROIX du BAC.	Sick Officers NIL other rank 33. Wounded — 2 — 6. A.D.M.S. inspected 19th & 82nd Field Ambulances also visited Rail Station. Instructions issued to all ambulances as to system of carrying through cases being taken by an Cars. Various sides inspected for re-arrangement of Field Ambulances.	
11th July 1915.	Sick Officers 1 other rank 37. Wounded — NIL — 7. O.C. Field Ambulances conducted round their new areas. R.D.M.S. inspected a new site for the 82nd Field Amb.	

Army Form C. 2118.

WAR DIARY
or
INTELLIGENCE SUMMARY.
(Erase heading not required.)

Hour, Date, Place	Summary of Events and Information	Remarks and references to Appendices
12th July 1915	Sick officers 2 Otherranks 33 Wounded "" NIL " 16 Visit of D.D.M.S. who informed A.D.M.S. of impending change in Divisional Area. A.D.M.S. visited Rest Station in STEENWERCK which will remain an area when change takes place.	
13th July 1915	Sick officers 1 Otherranks 25. Wounded " 1 " 8. Orders from Headquarters & names our line to be moved to the right with two Brigades in trenches and two in reserve. Field Ambulance positions altered as follows:- 2nd Fd. Amb. STEENWERCK with advanced Dressing station at ERQUINGHEM. 81st Fd. Amb. at HOLLEBEQUE. 19th Fd. Amb. FORT ROMPU. 19th Inf. Brigade will be relieved by 80th Bde and 81st.F.B. by 84th F.B. When these changes take place respective Field Ambulances will change over occupation of Advanced Dressings and continue reading with their own Brigade.	

Army Form C. 2118.

WAR DIARY
or
INTELLIGENCE SUMMARY.
(Erase heading not required.)

Instructions regarding War Diaries and Intelligence Summaries are contained in F.S. Regs., Part II. and the Staff Manual respectively. Title pages will be prepared in manuscript.

Hour, Date, Place	Summary of Events and Information	Remarks and references to Appendices
13th July 1915 Bailleul	STEENWERCK to be held eventually as a Divisional Rest Station by 2 Sections of Field Ambulances.	JM
14th July 1915 CROIX du BAC	Sick officers 1 other ranks 65 wounded — " — Nil 8 R.D.M.S. investigated question of Bath at STEENWERCK. Accommodation Nil at present. Orders concerning movement of adjacent Division not yet published — this rendered it impossible to time moves of Ambulances to new billets. R.D.M.S. interviewed D.D.M.S. on the subject. Capt. A.V. Raybury reported his arrival & posted to 83rd Field Ambulance. He resigned work of this officers. He freed Ambulance. It in consequence desirable, from point of view of seniority within Unit, that officers should return to their own Unit.	JM

WAR DIARY
or
INTELLIGENCE SUMMARY.

Army Form C. 2118.

Hour, Date, Place	Summary of Events and Information	Remarks and references to Appendices
15th July 1915. CROIX du BAC.	Sick officers Nil other ranks 37 wounded " " 1 " " 5. Following main carried out Std. Yd. Amb., 1 section and Field Station from BAC ST MAUR to STEENWERCK and one section to FROUINGHEM. 19th Fld. Amb. from FROUINGHEM to FORT ROMPU. Field Amb. workshops to STEENWERCK. Visit from D.A.D.M.S. 50th Div – a/ADMS. 8th Division & D.D.M.S. re moves. A.D.M.S. inspected positions of affairs at the various new billets.	JW
16th July '15	Sick officers 3 other ranks 47. wounded " " Nil " " 14. A.D.M.S. and A.A.Q.M.G. inspected FORT ROMPU. A.D.M.S. afterwards proceeded to STEENWERCK in reference to arrangement of Divisional Rest Station there.	JW
17th July '15	Sick officers 1 other ranks 45. wounded " " Nil " " 5.	JW

WAR DIARY
or
INTELLIGENCE SUMMARY.
(Erase heading not required.)

Army Form C. 2118.

Hour, Date, Place	Summary of Events and Information	Remarks and references to Appendices
18th July 1915 CROIX du BAC.	Sick officers 3 other ranks 60 wounded " " NIL " " 1 The 27th Division came under orders of 1st Army from 12 noon today. Reference to Daily reports of sick and wounded 1st Army begins hereafter if such to change. The only information of strength available to A.D.M.S. though it is not accurate & probably always in excess of reality. JM	[A.D.M.S. 27th DIVISION stamp] No. _____ Date _____
19th July 1915	Sick officers 1 other ranks 63 wounded " " NIL " " 5 One Field Ambulance relieves 19th Fd Ambulance at FORT ROMPU & takes over charge of right half of line 3rd Fd. Ambce are in charge of the left half of line and Run Red. Station. 8 Fd. Fd. Ambce. are act from their own Brigade and Divisional Batts Sick Ambulance to take charge of the section of line occupied by Reinforcement No 7 M.A.C. MERVILLE to Colonel Forth Forwarded to Divisional Order leaving of 1st Cav. Div. JM	

Army Form C. 2118.

WAR DIARY
or
INTELLIGENCE SUMMARY.
(Erase heading not required.)

Instructions regarding War Diaries and Intelligence Summaries are contained in F. S. Regs., Part II. and the Staff Manual respectively. Title pages will be prepared in manuscript.

Hour, Date, Place	Summary of Events and Information	Remarks and references to Appendices
20th July 1915. CROIX du BAC.	Sick officers Nil. Other ranks 61 Wounded " Nil " " 3 Reference re knitting and other measures for the coming winter. R.D.M.S. interviewed Capt. Potter 8 M Field Ambulance reference his complaint of being exposed, his O.C. being unsympathetic. Genl. difficiency is experienced in keeping the ditches of this country in a sanitary condition, owing principally to the fact that there is no slope, a fall in the ground. 19th Field Ambulance leaves 27th Divn and join 8th Division.	M
21st July 1915.	Sick officers Nil. Other ranks 47 Wounded " Nil " " 5 A.D.M.S. inspected all Field Ambulances including Advanced Post of 3rd Field Ambulance at Le GRIS POT.	M

Army Form C. 2118.

WAR DIARY
or
INTELLIGENCE SUMMARY.
(Erase heading not required.)

Instructions regarding War Diaries and Intelligence Summaries are contained in F.S. Regs., Part II. and the Staff Manual respectively. Title pages will be prepared in manuscript.

Hour, Date, Place	Summary of Events and Information	Remarks and references to Appendices
2nd July 1915 CROIX du BAC	Sick officers 3 other ranks 33 wounded — 1 other rank 4. Three reinforcement Medical officers Rank & JC arrived. Capt P.wood to 6th Field Amb. Capt J.C. Robb to 9th F.D. Amb. and Lieut J.C. Dunn who was sent on to join 19th Fd Ambulance 8th Divn. G.O.C. inspected Advanced Unit D.M.S. 1st Army visited Divisional Rest Station with a view to considering its value for continuation.	M
3rd July 1915	Sick officers 1 other ranks 39 wounded — 1 — 5. A.D.M.S worked Casualty Clearing Station at MERVILLE and No 5 Stationary Laboratory. Invited out to "Q" that if any extensive shrubbing or bread ations to be undertaken for the winter the present hundred dipping for Lahore need be stopped.	M

Army Form C. 2118.

WAR DIARY
or
INTELLIGENCE SUMMARY.
(Erase heading not required.)

Instructions regarding War Diaries and Intelligence Summaries are contained in F.S. Regs., Part II. and the Staff Manual respectively. Title pages will be prepared in manuscript.

Hour, Date, Place	Summary of Events and Information	Remarks and references to Appendices
29th July 1915 CROIX du BAC	Sick officers Nil Other ranks 40 Wounded -- Nil -- -- Nil -- A.D.M.S visited Advanced Dressing Station and Hd Qrs of 82nd Brigade.	[stamp: A.D.M.S. 27th DIVISION] JM
30th July 1915	Sick officers Nil Other ranks 58. Wounded -- Nil -- -- 1 -- Conference of D.M.S. 1st Army re methods of disposal of sick & wounded. Area Inoculation Scheme practicable to be adopted. Some Ambulances in action at LE TREE Ambulance.	JM
31st July 1915.	Sick officers Nil Other ranks 36 Wounded -- Nil -- -- 4 -- Visited STEENWERCK about improving condition of surface drains in vicinity of billets. The want of fall in the country results in stagnation of ditch water & ditches in dry weather. A.D.M.S. A.V. Maybury proceeded to H.Q. Corps. A.D. Field Ambulance for duty.	JM

WAR DIARY
or
INTELLIGENCE SUMMARY.

(Erase heading not required.)

Army Form C. 2118.

Hour, Date, Place	Summary of Events and Information	Remarks and references to Appendices
27th July 1915. CROIX du BAC	Sick officers Nil other ranks 40. Wounded — Nil — — 13. Lieut. Col. A.A. Martin of 82nd Field Ambulance interviewed. A.D.M.S. selected sites for future bathing arrangement.	[initials]
28th July 1915.	Sick officers 2 other ranks 48. Wounded — 1 — — 2. Readqrs & 1 Section of No 2 Mountain Battery leave the Division.	[initials]
29th July 1915.	Sick officers Nil other ranks 34. Wounded — Nil — — 1. Trenches at BOIS GRENIER inspected. Arranged for thermos of spraying by troops as a fly preventative. Sanitation fairly good all round, except water supply. Shallow wells in ground. purification uncertain.	[initials]

Army Form C. 2118.

WAR DIARY
or
INTELLIGENCE SUMMARY.
(Erase heading not required.)

Instructions regarding War Diaries and Intelligence Summaries are contained in F. S. Regs., Part II. and the Staff Manual respectively. Title pages will be prepared in manuscript.

Hour, Date, Place	Summary of Events and Information	Remarks and references to Appendices
30th July 1915. CROIX du BAC	Sick officers NIL other ranks 42. Wounded — NIL — S: Inspected trenches CHAPPELLE-ARMENTIERES. Sanitation of Glosters Ind., 9th Royal Scots Fus. & 1st Royal Irish very good. Devised order re cooking arrangement and flies.	AMS
31st July 1915. CROIX du BAC	Sick officers NIL other ranks 34. Wounded — NIL — 7. Evacuations now extraordinarily low. Monthly returns duly rendered. Inoculation State officers 98.7. other ranks 97.7.	

E.G. Moore
Colonel AMS
A.D.M.S. 27th Division

J. Wapound
Lieut Colonel
D. a. m. s. 27th

[Stamp: A.D.M.S. 27th DIVISION]

DIVISIONAL ROUTINE ORDERS, No. 32.

by

Major General T.D. Snow, K.C.B. Commanding 27th Division.

2nd July, 1915.

197. PREVENTION OF FLIES.

Crude paraffin will be issued at Refilling Point from 3rd July. Units should obtain this supply, and use it for the prevention of flies, especially round about the trenches. I should also be sprinkled frequently over all rubbish and manure heaps awaiting destruction by burning, and all areas of fouled ground in vicinity of billets and trenches.

The supply of Chloride of Line will be somewhat less than heretofore, but the extra paraffin will more than make up this deficiency if suitably used.

This order in no way affects the present distribution and use of cresol.

198. INTERPRETERS.

Interpreters will report to the Liaison Officer for their pay at Divisional Headquarters either on June 3rd or July 4th, between the hours of 2 and 5 p.m.

199. TRANSPORT.

Only one man besides the driver is allowed to ride on a loaded wagon.

200. INDENTS ON 2ND ARMY WORKSHOPS.

The 2nd Army Workshops at ARMENTIERES are now turning out and can issue to Divisions in the 3rd Corps the following:-

      Bayonet Periscopes.
      Loophole Periscopes.
      Rifle Grenade Aiming Rests.
      Sniperscopes.

Indents for these should be submitted through the C.R.E.

201. ROAD TRAFFIC.

The road from the ARRET in square I 8 a isxxkxxxd and from the ARRET in square I 9 b to the cross roads in I 9 c is closed for wheeled traffic during the hours of daylight.

H.J.EVERETT, Colonel,

A.A.& Q.M.G. 27th Division.

DIVISIONAL ROUTINE ORDERS, No. 36.

by

MAJOR GENERAL T.D'O. SNOW, K.C.B., Commanding 27th. Division.

6th. July, 1915.

223. DISCIPLINE.
(1) In accordance with para 583 King's Regulations, the Major General, Commanding the Division calls attention to the fact that the following crimes are unusually prevalent in certain units, viz:- Sleeping on his post, Striking or threatening Superior Officer and Disobedience to Superior Officer.
He directs that Section 6 (1) k, Section 8, and Section 9 of the Army Act be read out to the men on parade. Commanding Officers will so arrange parades that every man in their unit shall be present at one time or the other when these sections are read out.
(2) N.C.Os and men are forbidden to take liquor out of estaminets to their billets or to any other place.

(3) Estaminets in the town of Armentieres and its neighbourhood are open for the sale of liquor from 12 noon to 8 p.m. The G.O.C. will be compelled to curtail these hours unless there is a marked diminution in the crime of drunkenness.

(4) Whenever crime is unusually prevalent in a unit, Commanding Officers will detail extra piquets to patrol the neighbourhood of their billets.

224. DRINKING WATER.
Great difficulty is experienced in providing an adequate supply of drinking water in ARMENTIERES. Drinking water is laid on to houses and street fountains. Water for washing clothes and for all purposes other than drinking and cooking will be drawn from pumps.
Care must be taken to turn off taps after use.

225. SMOKE HELMETS.
(a) Attention is directed to Circular Memorandum issued herewith.

(b) Smoke Helmets which have been subjected to influence of gas shells, but not to that of gas from cylinders, need not be withdrawn for re-impregnation, as gas from the shells does not act on them chemically. (3rd.Corps G/2889/15. 27th.Division 1606/6).

226. RIFLES - RETURN OF TO BASE.
Ordnance, Base, reports that consignments of rifles returned have not been labelled to show from what unit, or under what authority. This must be carefully followed in despatching future consignments. (3rd.Corps Q/3857/15. 27th.Division No.1952.)

227. MOTOR VEHICLES.
When passing a parked convoy, all motor vehicles will slow down to 15 miles per hour.
(C.R.O. 202).

228. HAWKERS.
Hawkers are not allowed in the vicinity of Camps and Billets unless in possession of a "permit" signed by an A.P.M. stating the area they may frequent, and the goods they may sell. They are not to enter Billets or Camping Grounds.
All sentry and police posts are to be warned of this order.
(C.R.O.203.)

P.T.O.

229. **LEAVE. TRAIN AND BOAT SERVICE.**

The following special train and boat services for Officers and other ranks proceeding and returning from leave commenced on July 4th:-

		p.m.			p.m.
Steenwerck.		4-21	Victoria.	dep.	7-15 & 7-30
Bailleul.		4-38	Boulogne	arr.	11-30
Strazeele		4-50			a.m.
Hazebrouck		5-1	Boulogne	dep	1-48 a.m.
Ebblinghem		5-24	St Omer		4-25.
St Omer		5-44	Hazebrouck		5-40
Boulogne	arr.	9-00	Bailleul		6-19
		a.m.	Steenwerck		6-26.
Boulogne	dep	1-00			
Folkestone	dep	3-00			
Victoria	arr.	5-00			

Only General and Staff Officers may travel by the ordinary packet boats from BOULOGNE and CALAIS. All other Officers, N.C.Os and men must travel by the special leave boat.

Officers, N.C.Os and men proceeding to England on leave are always to give their address " before leaving their unit.

Divisional Routine Order, 215 of 4th. July is cancelled accordingly.

In case of absence the adress as well as the description of the man and date of absence will be forwarded to the A.P.M.

H.J. EVERETT. COLONEL.

A.A. and Q.M.G. 27th. Division.

DIVISIONAL ROUTINE ORDERS, No. 48.

by

MAJOR GENERAL G.F.MILNE, C.B., D.S.O., Commanding 27th. Division.

19th. July, 1915.

291. BATHS.
Divisional Routine Order No.33 of 4th.June, is cancelled and the following substituted. The Divisional Baths at ERQUINGHEM are allotted as follows from Tuesday next the 20th.instant:-

Sundays. -------- 80th.Infantry Bde. & 1st Brigade R.F.A.
Mondays. -------- 81st Infantry Bde. & 19th.Brigade R.F.A.
Tuesdays -------- 82nd.Infantry Bde. & 20th.Brigade R.F.A.
Wednesdays.-----(Remainder of Artillery in Divisional Area.
                (Divisional Units.
Thursdays -------80th.Infantry Bde. & 1st Brigade R.F.A.
Fridays. --------81st.Infantry Bde. & 19th.Brigade R.F.A.
Saturdays -------82nd.Infantry Bde. & 20th.Brigade R.F.A.

Parties for bathing will arrive at the following hours:-
8-45 a.m., 10-45 a.m., 2 p.m., & 4 p.m.
Parties are not to exceed 250 men. Men bring their own towels.
All clothing is ironed and change of underclothing is provided.
The O.C.Baths is to be informed on the previous day of the numbers of men whom it is proposed to bathe.
At present, the ERQUINGHEM baths are the only ones now working in the Divisional Area.

292. HAND GRENADES.
It is impossible at present to supply spare detonators for the No. 1 Hand Grenade without interfering with the supply of the complete grenade. Every endeavour should therefore be made to prevent the detonators being lost.
(W.O.121/Stores/2493 (A.3.) dated 9-7-15. - 0.567).

293. DIVISIONAL BAND.
The G.O.C. has approved of a divisional band being formed.
The following instruments are already available:-
1 Flute, 1 Piccolo, 1 Clarionet E b, 8 Clarionets B b, 5 Cornets, 4 French Horns, 1 Baritone, 1 Euphonium, 2 Tenor Trombones, 2 Basses E b, 1 Bass B b, 1 Side Drum, 1 Bass Drum, and 1 pair Cymbals.
O.C. Units will send in through the usual channels the Names of any N.C.O's they can recommend for the post of Bandmaster, also the names of any men they can recommend as trained bandsmen stating their qualifications, the instrument they can play, and their previous experience.

294. BAGGAGE WAGONS.
The practice of using Baggage Section Wagons of the Train for carting manure is strictly prohibited.

295. RATIONS.
It is notified that the following alterations have been made in the scale of rations:-
1 lb Fresh Meat instead of 1½ lbs or ⅝ lb (nominal) Preserved meat instead of 1 lb nominal.
When available condensed milk will be issued in the place of this reduction at the rate of 1 tin milk to every 8/10 men.

P. T. O.

296. **HUTTING ACCOMMODATION.**
With the exception of the 80th. Infantry Brigade, Officers Commanding Units in reserve will submit a return at once through the usual channels showing, after taking into account existing billeting accommodation, the number of Officers, N.C.O's, men and animals, for whom hutting accommodation and shelters will be required during the winter months, on the supposition that they occupy their present billets.

The Infantry Brigades in the trenches will only submit returns for their battalions in reserve.

This order applies to all units billeted in the 27th. Divisional Area whether they are Corps or Army Troops.

297. **FORAGE.**
The scale of rations for mules is as follows:-

Mules of 15 hands and upwards)
employed on heavy draught work)   Oats 12;   Hay 12.

Small Mules   Oats 6;   Hay 12.

Units will state on their ration indents (A.B. 55) the number of small mules on their strength.

298. **FIELD CASHIER.**
Reference Divisional Routine Order No.190 of 1st July; in column 3 for the address at Armentieres road:-
Blanchisserie de la Lys - ERQUINGHEM. (East End).

299. **STAFF.**
Captain G.R.F.Leverson, Nothumberland Fusiliers is appointed D.A.Q.M.G. of the Division with effect from 18th, July, 1915, vice Major W.E.T.Christie, A.S.C. appointed A.Q.M.G. II Corps.

300. **SMALL ARM AMMUNITION.**
All S.A.A. in the subsidiary line is to be collected together and stored in dug outs. Brigadiers Commanding Sectors of the defence line will report where these dumps are and the amount of ammunition in each.

301.   CANCELLED.

302. **SANITATION.**
Attention is called to the sanitary condition of billets and bivouacs.

There are too many old tins and scraps left lying about.

Officers Commanding Units are held responsible for the cleanliness of their billets and bivouacs and their surroundings.
Staff Captains will report any neglect of this kind to their Brigadiers.

303. **INOCULATION.**
The results of inoculation as affecting the Expeditionary Force up to 22nd. May,1915, have now been published and show that the ratio of attacks has been 14 times greater among the UNinoculated, and the ratio of deaths 42 times greater among the UNinoculated.

If UNINOCULATED a man is 14 times more likely to get TYPHOID, and 42 times more likely to die from typhoid than an inoculated man.

304. **FIELD AMBULANCES.**
Medical Units are now located as follows:-

    81st Field Ambulance - STEENWERCK.
    82nd. Field Ambulance - Rosary Farm B 26 b.
Dressing Station for right half of line FORT ROMPU, H 7 d.
    83rd. Field Ambulance - HOLLEBEQUE FARM in B 20 c.
Dressing Station for left half of line at ERQUINGHEM in H 4 d
                                                                              3.7

Reference 1/40,000 Map.

These dispositions will for the present be maintained.
The allocation of Field Ambulances to Brigades which has lately been in force, namely:-
    83rd. Field Ambulance to 80th. Brigade
    81st. Field Ambulance to 81st Brigade.
    82nd. Field Ambulance to 82nd. Brigade. will be maintained as far as possible in the present circumstances.

305. **MOVEMENTS BY RAIL.**
Owing to change of Railhead, all departures and arrivals by rail, except by the special LEAVE trains, will be carried out at LA GORGUE.
The daily special leave train will depart from and arrive at STEENWERCK as usual.

                                                H.J. EVERETT, COLONEL.
                                  A.A. and Q.M.G. 27th. Division.

DIVISIONAL ROUTINE ORDERS, No. 59.

by

MAJOR GENERAL G.F. MILNE, C.B., D.S.O., Commanding 27th. Division.

30th. July 1915.

367. CLAIMS FOR DAMAGES.
It has been brought to notice that claims for breakages and preventable damage are constantly being referred to the President, Claims Commission for adjustment. It is pointed out that although the Claims Commission has been appointed to investigate claims lodged by the inhabitants, it can only adjust those which are chargeable to the British Public.

2. With reference to General Routine Order No.634, General and other Officers Commanding will arrange that a claim shall, whenever possible, be brought home to the individual concerned and be dealt with by the Commanding Officer as a matter of discipline.

3. If, after investigation, it is decided by the proper authority that a claim or portion of a claim is chargeable to the public, or where the responsible individual cannot be traced, the claim should be dealt with by the General Officer Commanding if within his powers, or otherwise by the President, Claims Commission. See also General Routine Order No.763 dated 7th. April 1915.
(G.R.O. 1036).

368. WAR LOAN.
With reference to special Army Order dated 6th July, 1915, regarding the method in which soldiers serving in this country are to apply for War Loan, all Officers sending in these applications will, at the same time, forward a duplicate copy of Army Form W. 3144 to the Staff Paymaster i/c Clearing House, Base.
(G.R.O. 1045).

369. APPOINTMENTS.
(1) 2nd. Lieutenant J.J.B. Gaffney is appointed Adjutant 1st. Battalion Royal Irish Regiment, vice Captain A.H. Caldecott whose tenure of the appointment has expired, with effect from July, 27th, 1915.

(2) The following officers performed the duties of Adjutant, 1st Battalion Toyal Irish Regiment between the dates stated:-

2nd. Lieutenant N.A.H. Fox, 1st. Battalion Royal Irish Regiment, from June 17th till June 24th, 1915.

Captain H.G. Grogorie, 1st Battalion Royal Irish Regiment from June 25th. 1915, to July 26th. 1915.
(C.R.O. 216).

370. FLIES.
In order to diminish the number of flies in the trenches, cooking and eating are not to take place in the trenches, if it can be avoided, but in rear of the parados behind.

371. Leave.
The attention of all concerned is directed to Circular Memorandum No.492, circulated to-day.

H.J. EVERETT. COLONEL.
A.A. & Q.M.G. 27th. Division.

NOTICE.

FOUND. In the horse lines of the 1st Wessex Field Coy. R.E. a large mule marked 131 on both hind hoofs. Owner apply to Officer Commanding the above unit.

27th Division

121/6787

ADMS 27th Division

Vol XIII

August 15

Summarised but not copied.
Dec. 1923

August 1915

A.D.M.S. 27th Div. Aug 1915.

(Part of)
"Apx. 4" has been
detached & filed
under "Sanitation"
21

Army Form C. 2118.

WAR DIARY
or
INTELLIGENCE SUMMARY.
(Erase heading not required.)

Instructions regarding War Diaries and Intelligence Summaries are contained in F.S. Regs., Part II. and the Staff Manual respectively. Title pages will be prepared in manuscript.

Hour, Date, Place	Summary of Events and Information	Remarks and references to Appendices
1st August 1915 CROIX du BAC	Sick officers Nil Other ranks 43 Wounded " " " NIL Visited Divisional Baths to arrange necessary accommodation to 2000 per day and amend present bid system to shower system.	M
2nd Aug '15	Sick officers 1 other ranks 31 Wounded " " Nil " " 10 One section of Col. the Ambulance on Division attached to 2nd Field Ambulance for instruction at SORT. ROMPU. Conference of R. Dn. M S at MERVILLE re evacuation of "B" Class men, dental cases etc. Divisional order re disinfectants	M I
3rd Aug '15	Sick officers 4 other ranks 5-3 Wounded " " Nil " " 14 Major Waites Capt. received today will be used for looking up water at nightfall in the trenches.	[signature]

Army Form C. 2118.

WAR DIARY
or
INTELLIGENCE SUMMARY.
(Erase heading not required.)

Hour, Date, Place	Summary of Events and Information	Remarks and references to Appendices
4th August '15 CROIX du BAC	Sick officers 2 other ranks 30 wounded " Nil " 6. Capt. G.O. Chambers R.A.M.C. was sent with Instructions issued to Bearer Ambulances to evacuate cases of Advanced wounded at the earliest possible moment. This is the result of visit of Consulting Surgeon to 2nd Army. Arrangements made for Dentist to attend one day in each week at Bearer Rest Station in order to cope with the large amount of dental work on hand. Capt. McDelgado return to Divisions from 2nd Canadian Group & has been posted to 101 Lowland as M.O. vice Lieut J.A. Fletcher, Ladies proceeds to 13th Divisions for duty	JM
5th Aug '15	Sick officers Nil other ranks 45 wounded " " Nil " 3 Major W.H. Lent, Revd. Park Reddeny arrive, Lieut Cox to 2nd Zeal Ambulance to Capt Dicks Zeal Ambulance temporarily	JM

Army Form C. 2118.

WAR DIARY
or
INTELLIGENCE SUMMARY.
(Erase heading not required.)

Instructions regarding War Diaries and Intelligence Summaries are contained in F.S. Regs., Part II. and the Staff Manual respectively. Title pages will be prepared in manuscript.

Hour, Date, Place	Summary of Events and Information	Remarks and references to Appendices
6th August '15 CROIX du BAC	Sick officers nil other ranks 27 wounded nil " " 8 Dentist attends at Divisional Rest Station. Capt. C.H. Gregory 2nd 2nd Anzac enemies with a "B" men inspected at Rest Station. Col. Capt. R.O.S. Murray arrives posted to 2nd Field Ambulance. Divisional Orders re water supply handed over re population reputed in Divd. Order.	II JM
7th Aug '15	Sick officers 2 other ranks 80 wounded nil " " " " Examined Tolnet made by Sanitary Section inspected with a view to establishing an efficient means of evacuation of feces. R.D.M.S. visits G.S.F.B.	JM
8th Aug '15	Sick officers nil other ranks 71. wounded nil " " 8 Lieut. W.F. Baird + B. Borland arrive + reported for duty. to 1st + 8th Divisions respectively.	JM

Army Form C. 2118.

WAR DIARY
or
INTELLIGENCE SUMMARY.
(Erase heading not required.)

Instructions regarding War Diaries and Intelligence Summaries are contained in F.S. Regs., Part II. and the Staff Manual respectively. Title pages will be prepared in manuscript.

Hour, Date, Place	Summary of Events and Information	Remarks and references to Appendices
9th August 1915 CROIX du BAC	Sick officers 1st Ok ranks at 3 wounded — nil — — — Lieut. E.N. Graham to England on expiry of contract	M
10th Aug 15	Sick officers 3 other ranks 45 wounded — 1 — " — 5 Lieut. Davies to England on expiry of contract. Spraying of manure heaps is now being carried out in the area occupied by the sanitary section. Repeated inspection of trenches of 27th Div. Ambulance working well with exception of a medium for mixing with excreta. Lieut. R. A. J. Sheldon to relieve Lieut. F.G. Dickson on Medical officer 9th Royal Scots. Latter rejoin 1st Field Ambulance.	M

(stamp: A.D.M.S. 27th DIVISION)

WAR DIARY
or
INTELLIGENCE SUMMARY.
(Erase heading not required.)

Army Form C. 2118.

Hour, Date, Place	Summary of Events and Information	Remarks and references to Appendices
11th August 1915 CROIX du BAC	Other officers 1 other rank, the wounded ——— hit ———— Lieut Col R.P. Martin of R. A.M.C. Ambulance proceeded to Erquinghem. Major G.S. Wilton takes command of 82nd Field Ambulance. Divisional Order published re Convention of Brussels. He chief difficulty in the matter is the lack power of superv[is]ion of this district, which makes the disposal of wine very slow. Civilians are not available for large fits, now moved. Transport came back on registering therewith. Lieut R.N.T. Murray Roy 17th Ambl. proceeded to 5th Division for duty.	III
12th Aug/15	Other officers 1 other rank 45 wounded ———— at ———— Water supply in trenches. Have been supplied to the trenches for storage of drinking water. Taken direct from the R. [?]th Cart, where it is chlorinated. Have to date, and rec[eive]d water supplies bring drunk by old and new men here & there.	9. Barney (Soldier)
		JM
		JM

WAR DIARY or INTELLIGENCE SUMMARY.

Army Form C. 2118.

(Erase heading not required.)

Instructions regarding War Diaries and Intelligence Summaries are contained in F.S. Regs., Part II. and the Staff Manual respectively. Title pages will be prepared in manuscript.

Hour, Date, Place	Summary of Events and Information	Remarks and references to Appendices
12th August 1915	Sick officers nil other ranks 46. Wounded nil nil. Visited by members of entomological society who bombed and that blew flies whilst pupae eggs laid on meat and after refuse, even change brined several feet deep. This account for the large number now in the trenches as most ??? of such refuse has taken place here. Ammunition as ?????? in most places here ??? here is not invested with 5% Creol.	JM
14th August 15	Sick officers nil other ranks 57 wounded nil 2 8. Thirteen useful reinforcement of 2nd Cheshires inspected by R.O.M.C. Many were unable to march home until for any service at the front, refused to battle to H??graphers. Demonstration of the use of oxygen breathing apparatus given to Brigade Machine Gun officers by Gas expert at ERQUINGHEM	JM

Army Form C. 2118.

WAR DIARY
or
INTELLIGENCE SUMMARY.
(Erase heading not required.)

Instructions regarding War Diaries and Intelligence Summaries are contained in F.S. Regs., Part II. and the Staff Manual respectively. Title pages will be prepared in manuscript.

Hour, Date, Place	Summary of Events and Information	Remarks and references to Appendices
15th August 1915 CROIX du BAC	Irish Officers 1 other ranks 5-3 wounded " 2 " 6. Weekly conference at Duncans Bar instituted, also conference of D.R.M.S. He retains of Field Ambulance now assuming some proportions the question is up for consideration with a view to relieving the number of Sick and return rendered by them.	JM
16th August '15	Sick officers nil other ranks 50 wounded " 1 " 2 Capt. K.D. Mackenzie (D.C.) arrived and posted to Fdt Field Ambulance	JM
17th August '15	Irish officers 1 other ranks 5-8. wounded " 2 " 5 Col. Irish Ambulance relieved 2nd Irish Ambulance at FORT ROMPU	JM

WAR DIARY or INTELLIGENCE SUMMARY

Army Form C. 2118.

Hour, Date, Place	Summary of Events and Information	Remarks and references to Appendices
18th August 1915 CROIX du BAC	Sick officers 1 other ranks 35 - wounded — nr — — nr — Lues ligated Constant replies at the Divisional Baths. Underclothing will now be boiled in weak cresol solution before being washed. Colonel R.S. Wallace Consulting Surgeon 1st Army visited with reference to speedy evacuation of perforating abdominal wounds, all such cases, unless marked as being sent to Casualty Clearing Station as early as possible. Memorandum on Prevention of Flies and Sanitation issued to all units in the Division.	AMS IV
19th August 1915	Sick officers 4 other ranks 40 wounded — nr — — nr — S. Capt W.E. Aslin and Lt Anne proceeded to England. Major W.T. Grant to No 4 Stationary Hospital for duty. Lt Col. W.S. Kirby RAMC deemed Divisional Sanitary Officer selected as an alternative role.	VIII

Army Form C. 2118.

WAR DIARY
or
INTELLIGENCE SUMMARY.
(Erase heading not required.)

Instructions regarding War Diaries and Intelligence Summaries are contained in F.S. Regs., Part II. and the Staff Manual respectively. Title pages will be prepared in manuscript.

Hour, Date, Place	Summary of Events and Information	Remarks and references to Appendices
20th August 1915. CROIX du BAC	Sick officers nil other ranks 45. Wounded " 1 " 2. Capt. C. Philip Raine proceeded to 20th Division for duty. General Orders, number of cases occurring; Christ measures are being adopted in regard to report from Field Ambulances as to cases of infection and subsequent steps with the R.A.M.	M
21st August '15.	Sick officers nil other ranks 43. Wounded " nil " 2.	M
22nd August '15.	Sick officers nil other ranks 35. Wounded " nil " 1. Lieut. J.L. Enright arrived for duty & to to 82nd Field Ambulance.	M

Army Form C. 2118.

WAR DIARY
or
INTELLIGENCE SUMMARY.
(Erase heading not required.)

Instructions regarding War Diaries and Intelligence Summaries are contained in F.S. Regs., Part II. and the Staff Manual respectively. Title pages will be prepared in manuscript.

Hour, Date, Place	Summary of Events and Information	Remarks and references to Appendices
23rd August 1915. CROIX du BAC	Sick officers 2 other ranks 44 wounded nil " " 5. Visited new trenches taken over on right of line. Commenced adapting the Brewery at BOIS GRENIER as Brigade ballesting Station for right section - Brewery in CHAPPELLE D'ARMENTIERES to be similarly taken over in case of attack. Capt. Mahun In KERCAMP C.S.W. left Hyphenhurn - (some) suspended denial but did an advance to Casualty Clearing Station. Divisional Order published re disposal of unfit.	
24th August 1915	Sick officers 1 other ranks 42 wounded " 1 " " 11 R.O.R. reports difficulty in obtaining certificate to obtaining of proper authority in obtaining evacuation of unfitted	

WAR DIARY
or
INTELLIGENCE SUMMARY.
(Erase heading not required.)

Army Form C. 2118.

Hour, Date, Place	Summary of Events and Information	Remarks and references to Appendices
25th August 1915 CROIX du BAC	Sick officers 1 other rank 447. Wounded -"- -"- 12. Defence scheme for Divisional area received. Advanced Dressing Station kept section moved to Rue Marie. Room in pavement.	M
26th August '15	Sick officers nil other rank 444. Wounded -"- 1 -"- 6. Rear of Anthoine notified from 98th Batt R.G.A. evacuated to No 7 Casualty Clearing Station. Diagnosed Enteric; not examined bacteriologically.	M
27th August '15	Sick officers 1 other rank 443. Wounded -"- -"- 6. Inspected 98th Batt R.G.A. — no evidence found among horses, no trace of carrier. Case of anthrax, slight, examined, all effects burned. Visited Car Clearing Station any Effects Rue Marie had been sent immediately to base. Enid.	M

WAR DIARY or INTELLIGENCE SUMMARY

Army Form C. 2118.

(Erase heading not required.)

Instructions regarding War Diaries and Intelligence Summaries are contained in F.S. Regs., Part II. and the Staff Manual respectively. Title pages will be prepared in manuscript.

Hour, Date, Place	Summary of Events and Information	Remarks and references to Appendices
27th Aug /15 Contd	Following I.C. officers arrived and posted as shewn:— Lieut Black from Sea and 53 Italian " " " — W.A. Leach "	M
28th August 1915	Sick officer 1 other ranks 27/5. Wounded — " " " 5. Enquire re Ammonia Remedy for Poisonous Gas, issued to all French Units: and that 10 ohms expensive Oxygen Cylinder Oxygen fumes at Red Post and Advanced Dressing Stn.	M
29th August /15	Sick officer 1 other ranks 42. Wounded — " " " 6. R.O.M.s. proceeded on leave. Conference D.D.M.S. Then L/Cpl D.L.S. found unfit for service at the front, and endorsed to be evacuated under G.R.O. 975.	M

WAR DIARY or INTELLIGENCE SUMMARY

Army Form C. 2118.

Hour, Date, Place	Summary of Events and Information	Remarks and references to Appendices
30th August 1915 CROIX du BAC	Sick officers 1 other ranks 40. Wounded — nil — . Inspected dugouts for aid post left section. These have been much improved lately. Visited FORT ROMPU which a view to improving accn. of vehicles. In and out Gate arranged. The issue of one blanket per man has now been approved.	M
31st August	Sick officers 1 other ranks 37. Wounded — nil — . 2nd Lt. Audrew relieves 82nd Fd Ambce in left section. 80th Field Ambce come out to Divnl Reserve. Reorganisation of Divisional Baths to take 2000 per diem. commenced. Divisional Order re establishment of Corps Fd Ambce unit, requiring a large output than the normal issue of 1 drum per week.	VI / M

Army Form C. 2118.

WAR DIARY
or
INTELLIGENCE SUMMARY.
(Erase heading not required.)

Instructions regarding War Diaries and Intelligence Summaries are contained in F. S. Regs., Part II. and the Staff Manual respectively. Title pages will be prepared in manuscript.

Hour, Date, Place	Summary of Events and Information	Remarks and references to Appendices
31st August 1915 Contd. CROIX du BAC	Bentley returns rendered. Sanitary Report to DDMS during the month we admits 6 cases of Typhoid Group 1 case of Anthrax 1 case of Dysentery fever 1 case of Measles. Sanitary condition of Divison and Billets remain important. Ready vaccination returns show that 99.2% of officers and 99.7% other ranks are fully inoculated.	[Stamp: A.D.M.S. 27th DIVISION] J Wakeman Bolowe Rowe for ADMS 27th Division (Absent on leave)

Divisional Order No. 388th of 2nd August, 1915.

DISINFECTANTS.

Disinfectants which arrive at refilling point are issued proportionally to all units. When, however, extra supplies are available these are handed to the Officer Commanding, 27th Divisional Sanitary Section, and Units who have special needs will apply to this Unit who will meet demands as far as possible. FORMALDEHYDE is now only supplied through the Officer Commanding 27th Divisional Sanitary Section.

DIVISIONAL ROUTINE ORDERS, No.66.

by

MAJOR GENERAL G.F. MILNE, C.B.,D.S.O., Commanding 27th. Division.

6th. August, 1915.

408. CONTINUANCE IN THE SERVICE.

Reference Divisional Routine Order 384 of 2nd August, the one month's leave will equally apply to men who have completed 13 years service and who re-engage for 21 years. (A.G., G.H.Q. No.B.2055 dated 2-8-15., 27th. Division 2186).

409. DIVISIONAL BAND.

The Band will play, weather permitting, during the week ending Saturday August 14th. as follows:-

Sunday, August 8th	9-15 a.m. & 10-45 a.m., 81st Infantry Brigade Church Services.	
" " "	3.p.m. Steenwerck - Church Service.	
Monday " 9th	3.p.m. JESUS Farm (A 26 d 4.0).	
Tuesday " 10th.	3.p.m. Fort ROMPU (H 8 c 3.4).	
Wednesday " 11th.	3 p.m. JESUS Farm.	
Thursday " 12th.	ERQUINGHEM Bridge.(H 4.c 2.6) 3 p.m.	
Friday " 13th.	Jesus Farm. 3 p.m.	
Saturday. " 14th.	PETIT MORTIER (G.4 a 5.2). 3 p.m.	

410. LEAVE.

(a) The allotment of numbers of N.C.Os and men allowed to proceed on leave each week has, owing to the transfer of the 19th Infantry Brigade, been reduced to 210. This number is to be evenly distributed throughout the week i.e. 30 per diem

(b) Any Jewish soldier who would in the ordinary course be granted leave of absence during the next two months, may be permitted to select days including the 17th and 18th September(The Jewish "Day of Atonement").

411. WATER.

Attention is again directed to Divisional Routine Order No 109 dated 15th June.. Inspection reveals that many units are using unpurified water for drinking . No water obtained from wells or pumps in this district is fit for drinking without previous chlorination.

Tea need not be made with chlorinated water as the boiling is a sufficient purification.

Officers Commanding will treat all non-compliance of orders on this subject as serious breaches of discipline, and all ranks will cooperate to ensure compliance.

It is a mistake to say that present methods have not caused any ill-effects on health of men, the real reason for enforcement of water discipline is to protect the troops from ill-effects which may suddenly appear, and cause wide spread epidemic disease among them.

Chlorination can best be carried out in the water-carts and arrangements should be made that only water from this source is available for drinking.

412. Stationery Services.

The attention of all concerned is directed to General Routine Order No. 1048 dated 3rd instant regarding demands for Stationery &c.

P. T. O.

413. **TELEGRAMS.**
Telegrams of a personal or private nature are not to be sent through the signal service. This includes all telegrams to private addresses with reference to casualties or health of individuals.
(G.R.O. 1049).

414. **RATIONS.**
The special issue of Pea Soup authorized by General Routine Order No. 440 of 15-12-1914, will be discontinued for the present.
(G.R.O. 1052)

415. **SANITATION.**
Attention is again drawn to the instructions on the sanitation of billets issued with 1st Army Routine Orders No. 33 of 31-3-15, and subsequently with special reference to the prevention of prevalence of flies. Though in some cases these instructions have been carried out with excellent results, it is noticed that there are still many units in which the instructions are not being fully observed.
In view of the fact that the months of August and September are those in which flies, and the diseases due to their agency, become most prevalent, attention to preventive measures is now more than ever required. The most essential measures to be taken are the following:-
(1) The spraying of all manure heaps with a 5% solution of Cresol. One gallon of this solution per square yard of surface to be treated should be well sprayed over the surface of the manure heaps, in order to destroy eggs of flies which may have been laid there.
(2) The covering over of these manure heaps with earth, subsequent to spraying
(3) The immediate removal of all fresh manure to agricultural land at a distance from billets.
(4) The screening of all food from flies.
(5) The incineration of refuse of every kind, and of all latrine matter whenever this is possible.
(A.R.O. 102).

416. **PERSONNEL SENT TO BASE.**
It has been brought to notice that individual N.C.Os and men are frequently sent to the Base preceded by a telegram addressed to D.A.G., G.H.Q. 3rd. Echelon. If D.R.O. No. 208 dated 4th July is observed, such action is unnecessary.
With regard to N.C.Os and men about to be sent to the Base for discharge, until the procedure illustrated in Army Order XIII of 22-6-15 is in full working order, Officers Commanding Units should invariably refer to Officer i/c Records, 3rd Echelon, before accepting the statements of applicants for discharge as correct. In this connection attention is called to Divisional Routine Order No. 209 dated 4th July.

417. **HORSES.**
Horses exercising or going to water on the flats near the River LYS will invariably wear bits.

H.J. EVERETT, COLONEL.

A.A. & Q.M.G. 27th. Division.

DIVISIONAL ROUTINE ORDERS, No. 70.

by

MAJOR GENERAL G.F. MILNE, C.B., D.S.O., Commanding 27th. Division.

11th. August, 1915.

438. SANITATION.

Reference Divisional Routine Order No. 415 of 5th. instant, a certain number of sprayers and watering-cans are available at the Divisional Sanitary Section and will be sent round the various billets with men in charge for compliance with para 1 of above order.

439. INCINERATION OF EXCRETA.

In order to carry out the incineration of excreta a special form of latrine is necessary in which liquid and solid excreta are separated. A sample latrine and incinerator can be seen at the Sanitary Section, ERQUINGHEM, Square H.4 d 6.6.

All regimental medical officers and N.C.Os in charge of Sanitary Squads will see this plant in use.

Officers Commanding Units will then arrange for the construction of the plant in the vicinity of their bivouacs or billets. A man of the Sanitary Section R.A.M.C. can be detailed to help and direct in the construction.

The site for the plant will be selected in each case by the regimental Medical Officer.

It is desirable that these latrines should be as much concentrated as possible and that the plant should not be erected for less than one Company.

This work will be taken in hand at once.

440. RATIONS.

During the time that the cheese ration is reduced, fresh vegetables at the rate of $\frac{3}{4}$ lb. per ration may be purchased.

H.J. EVERETT. COLONEL.

A.A. and Q.M.G. 27th. Division.

The remainder of Appx. 4 has been filed separately

IV

DIVISIONAL ROUTINE ORDERS, No. 77.

by

MAJOR GENERAL G.F. MILNE, C.B., D.S.O., Commanding 27th. Division.

18th. August, 1915.

463. LEAVE.
With reference to para 3 of 1st Army Circular Memorandum No,15 of 15th. July, in which it lays down that leave for officers and men may be taken as meaning Monday to Monday etc.,etc.,both days inclusive, permission has now been obtained to interpret this order as follows:-
All Officers and Men. Leave will be reckoned as commencing on the day of departure from Boulogne and ending on the day of arrival at Boulogne.
Example. Leave from Sunday 22nd.August to Sunday 29th.August.

Leaves STEENWERCK .... 3-21 p.m. train Sunday 22nd August
(first day of leave)
-"- BOULOGNE .... 10 p.m. Sunday 22nd. August.

Arrives Victoria. .... 3 a.m. Monday 23rd. August.

Leaves Victoria . ... 5-40 p.m. Sunday 29th. August
(last day of leave)
Arrives BOULOGNE.....about 11-30 p.m. Sunday 29th. August.

Arrives STEENWERCK......... 6 a.m. 30th. August.

The above ruling will come into force from Sunday 22nd August inclusive.

464. TRAFFIC REGULATIONS.
(1) During the hours of daylight no formed bodies of troops larger than a platoon and only single wagons and motor vehicles will move south of a line running from CROIX DE ROME along RUE DELETTREE through L'ARMEE and RUE ALLEE to the cross road in square I 1 d,9.2.
All single motors or horsed vehicles moving south of the above line will do so at a slow pace to avoid raising dust.
(2) Infantry Brigades occupying the line will fix notice boards in the necessary positions.

465. SCHOOL OF MUSIC - APPOINTMENT.
The names of suitable Warrant Officers for the impending vacancy of Sergeant Major at the Royal Military School of Music, Kneller Hall, are required for selection.
Tact, good temper, activity, a liking for, and thorough understanding of the management of boys, in addition to strict sobriety are among the qualities necessary.
When submitting names, qualifications should be stated.

466. SMOKE HELMETS AND RESPIRATORS.
As some confusion exists owing to the variety of nomenclature used when describing or referring to certain components (mentioned below) pertaining to smoke helmets and respirators, it is notified for information that the following nomenclature should be used:-
Cases waterproof for helmets,
..   ..   for respirators.
Pockets for helmets.
Satchels for helmets.

P. T. O.

467. **RESPIRATORS**.
As soon as units receive their second smoke helmet the respirators will be returned to the D.A.D.O.S., 27th. Division.
The certificate as regards respirators issued on May 28th will then be discontinued.

H.J. EVERETT, Colonel.
A.A. and Q.M.G. 27th. Division.

NOTICE.

LOST. A pocket case, containing a cheque book and about 60 Francs, in the RUE MARLE on the 14th. instant.
Finder please return to Lieutenant Elder, 2nd. K. S. L. I.

DIVISIONAL ROUTINE ORDERS, No. 81.

by

MAJOR GENERAL G.F. MILNE, C.B., D.S.O., Commanding 27th. Division.

23rd. August, 1915.

481. DISCHARGES.
With reference to Circular Memorandum 27th. Div. No.2138 dated 18th July 1915, it is not proposed to send men to their homes in the Colonies before their time has expired (including the extra year for which they are liable).

Free passages are provided to Reservists who were residing in the Colonies on Mobilization; if the man elects to proceed at the first available opportunity after discharge, his discharge will be dated from the date of embarkation, but, if the man should wish to remain in this country for the extended period, he will be discharged as soon as possible after his arrival in England.

His return passage will, in this case, be allowed within six months from date of discharge, on application to the Officer i/c of Records.
(Authority W.O. letter No.19/Gen.No/5463 (A.G.2.B) Discharges. 27th Division No. 2168).

482. MEN PHYSICALLY UNFIT.
Men found unfit for duty at the front, though not suffering from any definite disease will be sent to the Divisional Rest Station for inspection by the A.D.M.S. who, if he concurs will class them as:-
    (A) Unfit for duty at the front.
    (B) Fit only for fatigue duties in the Divisional Area.
    (C) To be dealt with as Medical cases.

Those marked (A) will be returned to their units for despatch to the Base under G.R.O. No.975. (Authority to be quoted - C.R. 1868/50/A., D.A.G. 3rd.Echelon).

Those marked (B) will be returned to their units and remain until suitable employment can be found for them.

The A.D.M.S. will note his decision on the last page of Army Book 64, which must invariably be sent with the men to the Rest Station.

483. APPOINTMENTS.
It must be clearly understood that no further application to appoint officers who may be Company Commanders as Adjutants will be considered, and applications for Captains, other than Company Commanders are only to be forwarded under the most exceptional circumstances, which must be very fully explained.

484. CLOTHING - BATHS.
It is found that men are handing in "gift shirts" of light inferior texture at the Divisional Baths in exchange for Government shirts. This practice must cease. In future no clean shirt will be given to any man unless he hands in a government shirt.

485. NAILS.
When opening cases or boxes care is to be taken that nails are not left on roads or where there is any traffic as numerous casualties amongst horses have been caused by picked up nails.

P. T. O.

486. ARMY BOOK-395.

Any units not in possession of A.B. 395 will indent at once for them from the Base Stationery Depot, HAVRE.

487. HISTORICAL RECORDS.

The reports required under King's Regulations, paras.1930 to 1932, will not be required during the continuance of the campaign.
(G.R.O. 1097).

488. WAR DIARIES.

The duplicate copies of War Diaries kept in accordance with Field Service Regulations Part II., Section 140, will be forwarded to Officers in charge Records for safe custody, as confidential documents and for preservation, to be returned at the end of the War to the Officer Commanding the unit. As, however, Commanding Officers frequently desire to refer to recent entries in their diaries they may retain the duplicate copies for a period of three months before sending them to the Record Office.
(G.R.O. 1097).

H.J. EVERETT, Colonel.

A.A. and Q.M.G., 27th. Division.

NOTICES.

Lectures on the "Pyramids of Egypt" and "St. Peter's Rome" will be given this week at 6 p.m. as follows:-
Tuesday, at billet of 98 Coy A.S.C. (Divl.Train) A. 28 b.
Wednesday - at 27th Divisional Headquarters.
Thursday - at "A" Battery 53rd F.A. Bde. Farm. (H. 8. b).
Friday - at 81st Field Ambulance Steenwerck.

FOUND. Pocket book containing 3 five franc notes and envelopes addressed to Mrs. Bywater. Owner should apply to A.P.M. 27th.Division.

DIVISIONAL ROUTINE ORDERS, No. 89.

by

MAJOR GENERAL G.F. MILNE, C.B., D.S.O., Commanding 27th. Division.

31st. August, 1915.

526. **APPLICATIONS FOR TRANSPORT.**
Reference Divisional Routine Order No.365, when making application for transport units will state for what purpose they require the wagons.

527. **SMOKE HELMETS.**
The new pattern (tube) smoke helmet will be carried in the satchel, and the old pattern helmet in the pocket sewn under the flap of the Service Dress Jacket (27th Division No. 2356).

528. **REFILLING.**
On and after the morning of September 1st. 1915, refilling will take place at 9 a.m.

529. **CRESOL.**
An extra reserve of cresol has been placed with the Sanitary Section at their Headquarters, ERQUINGHEM. Infantry Battalions needing more than the normal supply of 5 gallons per week should apply for it from the Sanitary Section.
About one drum per fortnight can be drawn.

530. **LATRINES.**
Officers Commanding Units will take steps to see that all latrines are screened from view by the erection of screens

531. **STAINING OF TENTS.**
When it is found necessary to stain tents in use by the troops at the front, Cutch and Copper Sulphate mixture, which has given satisfactory results when experimented with at the Base, should be used. 6 ozs. of Cutch with $\frac{3}{4}$ ozs. copper sulphate dissolved in 2 gallons of boiling water is sufficient for staining one tent C.S.L. The mixture will be supplied on receipt of indents submitted through the usual channel. The directions for use are as follows:-
    (1) Lay the tent flat on the ground on its side.
    (2) Wet it thoroughly with water.
    (3) Apply the solution with a mop or brush.
    (4) Let it get nearly dry before turning the tent over to do the other side.
    (5) The solution should be applied hot.

                          H.J. EVERETT,   Colonel.
              A.A. and Q.M.G., 27th. Division.

NOTICE.

STOLEN - On the 17th. instant from outside the Battalion Headquarters of 5th. Loyal North Lancs, two bicycles:-
    (a) B.S.A. with back pedalling brake marked "No.1.1/5th. L.N.Lancs" on the frame and on the back mudguard. Red Glass reflector on back.

    (b) Similar to above but marked "No.3. 1/5th.L.N.Lancs in the same manner.

adms

27th Division

121/7/53

A.D.M.S. 27th Division
War
Sept 15

Summarised by not copied
Dec. 1923.

Sep '15
S

Maps have been detached from Sept. diary and attached to Summary

Army Form C. 211

WAR DIARY
or
INTELLIGENCE SUMMARY.
(Erase heading not required.)

Instructions regarding War Diaries and Intelligence Summaries are contained in F.S. Regs., Part II. and the Staff Manual respectively. Title pages will be prepared in manuscript.

[Stamp: A.D. 27th DIVISION]

Places	Date	Hour	Summary of Events and Information	Remarks and references to Appendices
CROIX du BAC	1/9/16	—	Sick officers nil O.R. 15 wounded — nil O.R. 1. Construction of Dug out at GRIS POT commenced and Brewery at BOIS GRENIER cleared out and prepared for use as an Advanced Dressing Station. The Brigade Referee Officers as detailed from each Field Ambulance warned as to their responsibility regarding Parade Prayers in Trenches being in working order and that supplies of solution are being kept up.	
"	2/9/16	—	Sick officers nil O.R. 17 wounded " nil O.R. 1. D. D. M. S. inspected Rail Station. Construction of alternative entrance road to FORT-ROMPU Dressing Station commenced.	
"	3/9/16	—	Sick officers nil O.R. 9 wounded — nil O.R. 1. Act. O.C. issued Ambulances and discussed details of collection of sick and wounded during action.	
"	4/9/16	—	Sick officers nil O.R. 21 wounded — nil O.R. it Visited all Medical Units.	

[Signature] Rawe
Captain
S.A. D.M.S

Army Form C. 2118

WAR DIARY
or
INTELLIGENCE SUMMARY.
(Erase heading not required.)

Instructions regarding War Diaries and Intelligence Summaries are contained in F. S. Regs., Part II. and the Staff Manual respectively. Title pages will be prepared in manuscript.

[Stamp: A.D.M.S. 27th DIVISION]

Place	Date	Hour	Summary of Events and Information	Remarks and references to Appendices
CROIX du BAC	5/9/15.		Sick officers 1 - O.R.s. wounded --- nil O.R.s ? Conference D.D.M.S. 2nd Field Ambulance moved into L'ESTRADE 3rd Field Ambulance instructed to gradually reduce the numbers held in the Divisional Rest Station.	
"	6/9/15.		Sick officers nil O.R.s 77. wounded --- nil O.R.s 4. Visited all Medical Units. Arranged with A.D.M.S. 8th Division and wrote him agreeing to collect casualties from the left Sub Sect at I.31 a. sheet 36. from midnight 7th until further notice. Lieut Colonel F.J. Brakenridge R.A.M.C. Rev. Orders ordered to join 17th Corps as D.A.D.M.S. Lieut. B. Wallace R.A.M.C. S.C. instructed to proceed to 6th Division for duty.	
"	7/9/15.		Sick officers nil O.R.s 33. wounded --- nil O.R.s 9. Alterations road at Dressing Station FORT ROMPU completed - also the Dug out at GRIS POT. Visited R.D.M.s 2nd Division re the attachment of details of Field Ambulance 2nd Div to 27th Div for instruction.	

G.P. Renton
Captain R.A.M.C.
D.S.D.M.S.

Army Form C. 2118

WAR DIARY
or
INTELLIGENCE SUMMARY.
(Erase heading not required.)

Instructions regarding War Diaries and Intelligence Summaries are contained in F. S. Regs., Part II. and the Staff Manual respectively. Title pages will be prepared in manuscript.

Place	Date	Hour	Summary of Events and Information	Remarks and references to Appendices
CROIX du BAC	8/9/15		Sick officers nil O.R. 26. Wounded --- nil O.R. 2. Details of 70th Field Ambulance 23rd Divn attached to 82nd Field Ambulance. Saw 'Q' about improvement of billeting accommodation at LESTRADE - for the wounded and visited actg escripts Lieut Col. O.C. Field Ambulance to discuss further details of defence scheme.	
"	9/9/15		Sick officers nil O.R. 17. Wounded " nil O.R. 1. Lieut. Col. J. J. Brakenridge R.A.M.C. proceeds to 17th Corps. Lieut. Col. J. Ward Rave D. of O. 8th Fd. Field Ambulance appointed acting A.D.M.S., temporarily in absence of A.D.M.S. in Leave. Divisional Order re cleaning of Barns for occupation as billets.	
"	10/9/15		Sick officers 1 O.R. 20. Wounded " nil " 1. Capt. G. S. Rudkin R.A.M.C. arrives in relief of Lieut. Col. J. J. Brakenridge as D.A.D.M.S. 27th Divn.	

V. Reyburn Capt R.A.M.C.
S.A.D.M.S.

Army Form C. 2118

WAR DIARY
or
INTELLIGENCE SUMMARY.
(Erase heading not required.)

Instructions regarding War Diaries and Intelligence Summaries are contained in F.S. Regs., Part II. and the Staff Manual respectively. Title pages will be prepared in manuscript.

A.D. 27th DIVISION (stamp)

Place	Date	Hour	Summary of Events and Information	Remarks and references to Appendices
CROIX du BAC	11/9/15		Sick officers nil O.R. 16. Wounded — nil O.R. nil. ADMS with ROs 23rd Divn visited all Advanced Dressing Stations, Fd. Ambs. and Rest Station. Inspected about 30 "old men" of 2nd K.O.S.b. & employing them for light duties — also inspected some men at Rest Station for same purpose.	
"	12/9/15		Sick officers nil O.R. 20. Wounded — nil O.R. nil. Conference D.D.M.S.	
"	13/9/15		Sick officers 2 O.R. 24. Wounded — nil O.R. 1. Medical Units, by close of 23rd Division — Chin after Operation orders issued for general relief of Consultation with R.D.M.O. 2nd Divn.	

V.P.S.M. Capt
ADMS

2353 Wt. W3H/1454 700,000 5/15 D.D. & L. A.D.S.S./Forms/C. 2118.

WAR DIARY
or
INTELLIGENCE SUMMARY.

(Erase heading not required.)

Army Form C. 2118.

Place	Date	Hour	Summary of Events and Information	Remarks and references to Appendices
CROIX du BAC	14/9/15		Sick officers 1 O.R. 26. Wounded — 1 O.R. 10. R.O.M.S returns from leave. 8nd Field Ambulance moves into 80th Brigade billets near MERRIS — after relief by 69th Field Ambulance 23rd Divn. The Field Ambulances are moving this time with mobilization equipment only. Extra Equipment – including Red Cross equipment etc. being handed over to medical Units 23rd Division on relief.	
	15/9/15		Sick officers 1 O.R. 50. Wounded — nil O.R. 5. 8nd Field Ambulance proceed with 80th Brigade to billets near STRAZEELE. Increase in evacuation sick due to move.	

J. Robertson Capt
R.A.M.C

Army Form C. 2118

WAR DIARY
or
INTELLIGENCE SUMMARY.
(Erase heading not required.)

Instructions regarding War Diaries and Intelligence Summaries are contained in F. S. Regs., Part II. and the Staff Manual respectively. Title pages will be prepared in manuscript.

Place	Date	Hour	Summary of Events and Information	Remarks and references to Appendices
MERRIS	16/9/15	—	Sick officers nil. O.R. 1 wounded — O.R.'s O.R. nil. R.A.M.C. name to MERRIS with H.Qrs. en route to new area. 17? Stretcher handed in to London Boundly Clearing Station today by Fd. Sick Ambulance, have had them used for patients as cot accommodation in Red Station. Major J.G. Bucknell RAMC Jr. rejoins Fd. Sick Ambulance from Sick Conv. Depot.	
"	17.9.15		Sick officers nil O.R. 27. wounded — Division adv. of action. 82nd Fd. Amb. move off and entrain for X— at THIENES with 80th Brigade. Fd. Sick and Fd. Amb. hand over to 70th Fd. Amb. and proceed to BISSEK near MERRIS with 81st Brigade. Fd. Sick and Amb and Sanitary Section warned as to line of entrainment and route pointed out to them. All motor Ambulances are being formed a convoy to proceed to new area by road, under officers of sanitary section. 1 Officer and 1 other of this Division left behind as patient in Rest Station	

W.R.S... Capn
ADMS

Army Form C. 2118

WAR DIARY
or
INTELLIGENCE SUMMARY.
(Erase heading not required.)

Instructions regarding War Diaries and Intelligence Summaries are contained in F. S. Regs. Part II. and the Staff Manual respectively. Title pages will be prepared in manuscript.

Place	Date	Hour	Summary of Events and Information	Remarks and references to Appendices
MERRIS	17/9/15 continued		Handed over to 33rd Division by rail as they became fit. O.C. 3rd Fld. Amb. 33rd Fld Amb & Sanitary Section taken over their route to the stations where they will entrain, in order to avoid a hitch.	
MERRIS	18/9/15	8am	No report sick – all units temporarily out of touch. A.D.M.S. moves to WARFUSEE-ABANCOURT. 33rd Field Ambulances arrive at GUILLACOURT – Advance and bivouac near MORCOURT on SOMME.	
WARFUSEE ABANCOURT		4pm	R.M.O. on arrival proceed to front area and arranged to relieve the French at Advanced Dressing Station CAPPY on night of 19/20th inst – Dressing Station to be established at FROISSY.	
"	19/9/15		Capt. R Griffiths R.A.M.C. S.R. arrived and posted to 33rd Field Ambulance for duty. R.M.O. inspect Regimental Aid Posts as used by the French – there will be used lines being used until relief is complete, subsequently changed as necessary.	

J. R. McCapron Captain
D.A.D.M.S.

Army Form C. 2118

WAR DIARY
or
INTELLIGENCE SUMMARY.
(Erase heading not required.)

Instructions regarding War Diaries and Intelligence Summaries are contained in F. S. Regs., Part II and the Staff Manual respectively. Title pages will be prepared in manuscript.

A.D.M.S. 27th DIVISION

Place	Date	Hour	Summary of Events and Information	Remarks and references to Appendices
WARFUSEE.	20/9/15		8th & 9nd Field Ambulances arrived and bivouac'd to MORCOURT and Bivouac for the night. A.D.M.S. select billets for 8th Field Ambulance in MORCOURT and 9nd Fd. Amb. in CHUIGNOLLES. R.D.M.O. inspect various sites for location of Divisional Bath – there are no suitable buildings in this area for the purpose.	
MERICOURT	21/9/15		R.D.M.S. moves to MERICOURT. 9nd Field Ambulance proceed to CHUIGNOLLES and staff the Advanced Dressing Station at CHUIGNES. 8th Field Ambulance open up as a Dressing Station in MORCOURT for sick of 9th Brigade in reserve area. 8th Field Ambulance Dressing Station and Headquarters move to LANEUVILLE. Sanitary Section established their Headqrs in MERICOURT.	
"	25/9/15		Wastage from sickness during move over 18th and 1- officers 1- O.R. 57- wounded officers nil O.R. 7. Conference at F. Amb (Div). R.O.Mrs render known and Unknown list for period April 22nd to 28th May – YPRES.	

J. P. Rawlins Captain
A.D.M.S.

Army Form C. 2118

WAR DIARY
or
INTELLIGENCE SUMMARY.
(Erase heading not required.)

Instructions regarding War Diaries and Intelligence Summaries are contained in F.S. Regs., Part II. and the Staff Manual respectively. Title pages will be prepared in manuscript.

Place	Date	Hour	Summary of Events and Information	Remarks and references to Appendices
MERICOURT	27/9/15		D.A.D.M.S. inspected trenches of 80th Brigade surveyed area for location of 81st Brigade Advanced Dressing Station. R.D.M.S. inspected various locations for location of Divisional Laundry.	
"	27/9/15		Sick officers nil O.R. 35 wounded " nil O.R. 2	
			Each Field Ambulance instructed to detail a medical officer to take charge of care for testing chemical fumes in water to be prepared to join up with Brigade Headquarters when required. R.D.M.S. 27th Division visit R.D.M.S. 17th Dn for instruction. Divisional order published re location of Medical Units	
"	28/9/15		Sick officers nil O.R. 37 wounded " nil O.R. 2	
			3rd Fld Ambulance move to Bilevue PROYART Anaesthetic Section move to Lieutenant LANEUVILLE Divisional order published re issue of solution	II

J.M. Ruskin Captain
D.A.D.M.S.

WAR DIARY or INTELLIGENCE SUMMARY

Army Form C. 2118

Place	Date	Hour	Summary of Events and Information	Remarks and references to Appendices
MERICOURT	7/9/15		Sick officers 1 O.R. 8. Wounded nil O.R. 1. Issue of Vermorel Sprayers 15 to each sector and arrangements made for each Advanced Dressing Station to keep supplies of sprayer solution for issue to units in trenches. 1 Vermorel sprayer also to each Field Ambulance and 1 spare one to Regt. Station. Lieut. Lawley R and SC transferred from 82nd Field Ambulance to 82nd Field Ambulance. Divisional order re sanitation	
"	10/9/15		Sick officers 1 O.R. 31. Wounded nil 1 O.R. 7. D.A.D.M.S. L.O.G. Sanitary Section made an inspection of the billets in CAPPY — numerous suggestions made to O.C. unit concerned. A.D.M.S. visited all Field Ambulances and gave verbal instructions re Emergency either to be carried in the motor Ambulances. Loose fodder only to be used for bedding fittings forms & furniture to be left behind in the event of a forward move.	

Army Form C. 2118

WAR DIARY
or
INTELLIGENCE SUMMARY.
(Erase heading not required.)

Instructions regarding War Diaries and Intelligence
Summaries are contained in F. S. Regs., Part II.
and the Staff Manual respectively. Title pages
will be prepared in manuscript.

Place	Date	Hour	Summary of Events and Information	Remarks and references to Appendices
MERICOURT	27/9/15	-	Sick officers nil O.R. 31 wounded — nil O.R. 8	
"	28/9/15	-	Sick officers 2 O.R. 37. wounded — 1 O.R. 10 R.M.O. visited all medical units and Road Stations	
"	29/9/15	-	Sick officers nil O.R. 42. wounded — nil O.R. 12 Hospital Barge arriving for use at Chr Division as a Hospital Grand Trunk Road Field Ambulance. The Barge to remain near FROISSY Bridge.	
"	30/9/15	-	Sick officers 2 O.R. 33 wounded — 1 O.R. 13 A.D.M.S. inspected Hospital Barge and handed it over to 82nd Field Ambulance. Arrangements made for laundry work of the Division to be carried out at BOVES. Soiled clothes Out Wd A.154 C.DMS C.DMS A.D.M.S Form C.2118 partial Bath MERICOURT, disinfected	A. M. Rusken Cpt

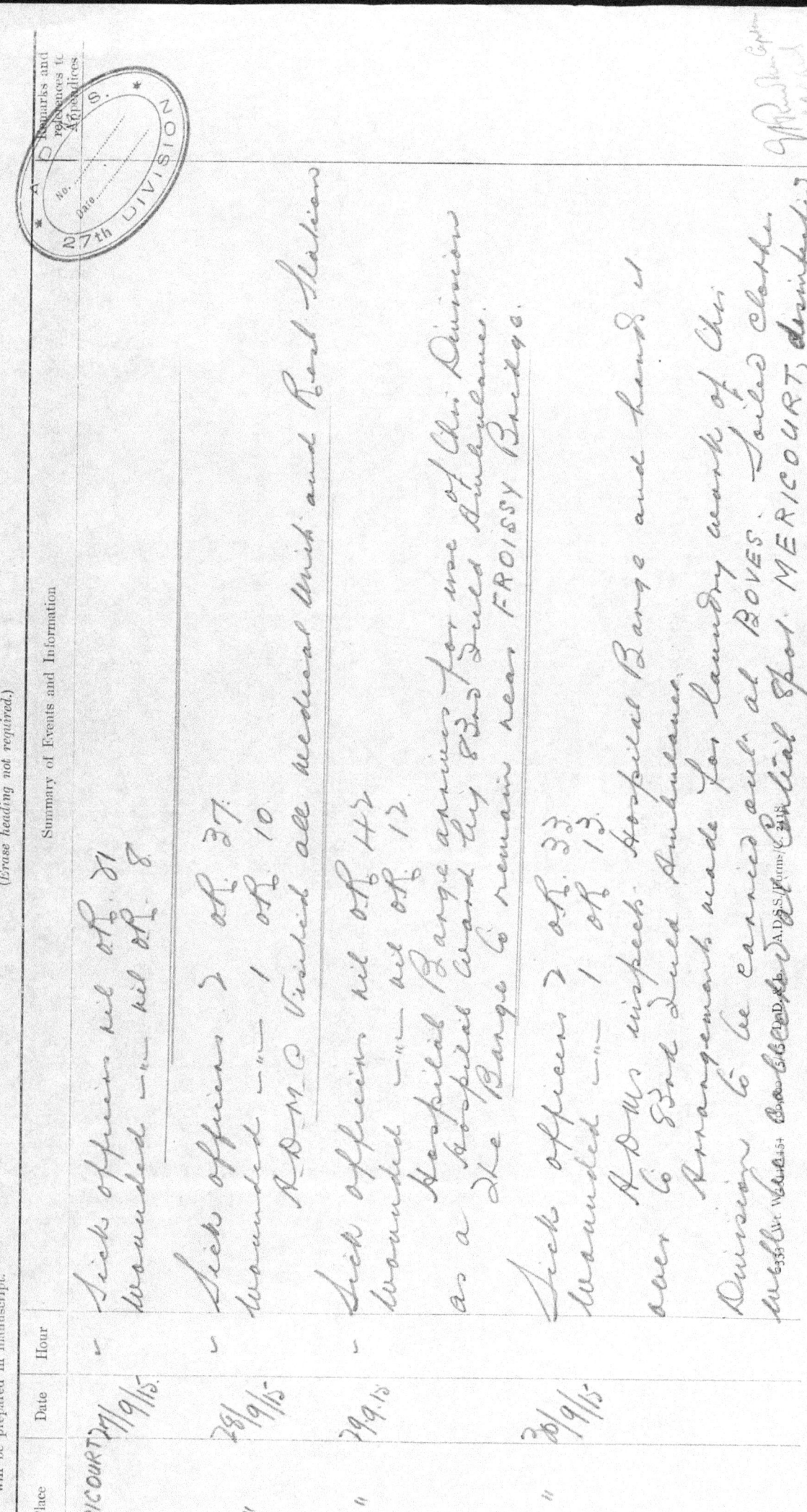

Army Form C. 2118

WAR DIARY
or
INTELLIGENCE SUMMARY.
(Erase heading not required.)

Instructions regarding War Diaries and Intelligence Summaries are contained in F. S. Regs., Part II. and the Staff Manual respectively. Title pages will be prepared in manuscript.

Place	Date	Hour	Summary of Events and Information	Remarks and references to Appendices
MERICOURT	30/9/15		In a Sheet Disinfector and despatched on a lorry to BOVES to be washed and mended.	
			Maps — two attached shewing area held by this Division on ARMENTIERES front, and also present front FRISE - DOMPIERE, and Divisional area to shew location of Medical Units etc. etc. Evacuation Return for September attached also. 1 Case of Enteric and 2 cases of Paratyphoid (T.A.I.B.) have occurred during the month.	

J.A. Rusby
Captain R.A.M.C.

E.G. Hopper
Colonel A.M.S.
A.D.M.S. 27th Divn

A.D.M.S. 27th Div.
Sept. 1915

MONTHLY INOCULATION RETURN.

27th Division. **September 1915.**

Unit.	Strength Offrs.	O.Rks.	Inoculated Offrs.	O.Rks.	Percentage Offrs.	O.Rks.	Numbers inoculated during month.
H.Q. Unit 27th Div.	15	70	15	70	100.	100.	
2nd K.S.L.I.	28	975	27	975	96.4	100	
3rd K.R.R.C.	25	988	23	984	92.0	96.5	6
4th K.R.R.C.	26	999	26	999	100	100	1
4th Rifle Bde.	25	1054	25	1027	100	92.3	4
P.P.C.L.I.	26	962	26	954	100	99.1	9
1st R. Scots	26	1005	26	999	100	99.4	
9th R. Scots	30	687	30	687	100	100	
2nd Glosters	26	1017	21	800	80.7	78.6	37
2nd Camerons	31	996	31	996	100	100	
1st A & S.H.	28	1007	28	1007	100	100	
1st R.I. Regt.	24	825	24	794	100	96.5	
2nd D.C.L.I.	25	963	23	955	92.0	99.1	
2nd R.I. Fusrs.	25	928	25	928	100	100	
1st Leinsters	26	887	26	887	100	100	
1st Cambs.	30	712	30	709	100	99.5	
H.Q. R.A.	4	24	4	24	100	100	
1st Brigade R.F.A.	25	752	24	751	96.0	99.8	
19th Bde. R.F.A.	25	733	25	724	100	98.7	
20th Bde R.F.A.	25	753	24	729	96.0	96.8	
129th Bde R.F.A.	4	132	4	132	100	100	
27th Divn. Am. Col. RFA.	17	526	15	514	88.2	97.7	
2nd Can. Hy. Bde RGA.	6	196	6	196	100	100	
82nd Trench Bty. RA.	2	23	2	22	100	95.6	
98th do do do	1	25	1	25	100	100	
27th Divn. Train ASC.	25	424	25	387	100	91.2	
27th Divn. Engrs.	27	806	27	791	100	99.4	
7th Labour Batt. RE.	2	249	2	246	100	98.7	
27th Div. Cyclist C.	7	198	7	198	100	100	
27th Divn. Yeomanry	6	136	6	136	100	100	
16th Mobile Vet. Sect.	1	28	1	28	100	100	
81st Fld. Ambce.	10	242	10	242	100	100	
82nd do do	10	237	10	235	100	99.1	
83rd do do	10	241	10	233	100	96.6	
27th Divn. San. Sect.	1	25	1	25	100	100	
27th Divn. F.A. Workshop Section.	1	19	1	19	100	100	
Total.	625.	19844.	611.	19428.	97.8	97.9	57.

H.Q. 27th Division.
30th September, 1915.

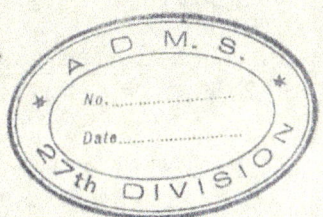

Colonel A.M.S.
A.D.M.S. 27th Division.

DIVISIONAL ROUTINE ORDERS, No. 110.

by

MAJOR GENERAL G.F. MILNE, C.B., D.S.O., Commanding 27th Division.

23rd September 1915.

621. DISCIPLINE. - Watering of Horses.
Instances have been brought to notice where horses are watered without proper supervision, causing congestion of roads and blocking traffic. All Watering order parades should be in charge of an Officer and carried out with proper system and due regard to march discipline.

622. ROAD CONTROL.
No motor cars except motor ambulances in very urgent circumstances are to go East of the line CAPPY-CHUIGNES.

623. MEDICAL UNITS.
Medical Units 27th Division will for the present be located as follows:-

 81st Field Ambulance. at MORCOURT with Medical Inspection at
  LAMOTTE, near the Church.

 82nd Field Ambulance. at CHUIGNOLLES with Advanced Dressing
  Station at CHUIGNES.

 83rd Field Ambulance. at LANEUVILLE (BRAY) near the bridge,
  with Advanced Dressing Station at CAPPY (near the church).

 Sanitary Section. at MERICOURT.

 Field Ambulance Workshops. at WARFUSEE-ABANCOURT.

The sick of Headquarters Unit will be seen at Medical Inspection Room located in the MAIRE - Moricourt at 8 a.m. daily.

624. DESPATCHES.
Reference para 2 Circular Memorandum No.2628 of 22nd.September, the recommendations for the period 28th May - 18th September will be sent in to this Office in order of merit in Artillery Brigades, R.E. Companies, Battalions etc., and not in a further compiled list as stated in last sentence of para 2 Circular Memorandum No.2611 of 14th September. G.Os.C. Infantry Brigades will only, for instance, pin together the lists in order of merit of their Headquarters and the 5 Battalions.

625. TOOLS.- Files old.
All unserviceable files are in future to be returned to the D.O.O. at Refilling Point. (3rd Army O/136, 27th Divn. O/715.)

626. TENTS - Painting of.
Reference Divisional Routine Order No.586 of 14-9-15, the scale of paint allowed for the colouring of tents is four lbs per C.S.L. Tent. The paint can be supplied in the proportions required, but the total weight allowed per tent is 4 lbs.

627. ARMY RESERVISTS.
It has been decided that Army Reservists cannot be permitted to extend their service, or to re-engage at present. It is open to such men to continue serving for the duration of the war, and the matter of their being allowed to re-engage will then be further considered.(W.O. letter No.27/Gen No./4655 (D/A.G.2.B.), 27thDiv.2632).

P. T. O.

628. **POSTINGS OF OFFICERS.**
A considerable number of cases are now occurring in which the departure of officers to take up appointments is delayed by the O.C. the Unit in which the Officer concerned is serving.
Steps will be taken to ensure that all such orders are carried out promptly, or that if any strong reason exists why the Officer's departure should be delayed, reference is at once made for sanction.
(A.G., G.H.Q.A/6831, 27th Division No. 2630.).

629. **INJURIES TO HORSES.**
(a) Considerable loss of efficiency occurs by horses picking up nails. Every care must be taken that nails are collected at places such as Refilling Points, R.E. Parks and Ordnance Depots where boxes are opened, and that they are not left lying about on the ground or remaining in the wood.
Wood used for fuel, especially in cookers on the road, is to be examined before use in order to see that all nails have been extracted.
(b) Attention is also directed to the number of instances of horses being injured by kicking one another.
It is quite understood that there are difficulties under present conditions in keeping horses separate, particularly where units are billeted in congested areas, but every care should be taken to segregate horses known to be kickers and to take all measures which will reduce the number of accidents of this nature.
(27th Division No. Q.189).

H.J. EVERETT, Colonel,
A.A. and Q.M.G.,   27th. Division.

DIVISIONAL ROUTINE ORDERS, No. 111.

by

MAJOR GENERAL G.F. MILNE, C.B.,D.S.O., Commanding 27th Division.

24th.September, 1915.

630. **DISPOSAL OF FIELD CONDUCT SHEETS (Army Form B.122).**
The attention of all concerned is directed to the footnote of Appendix IX Field Service Regulations Part II in connection with the disposal of Field Conduct Sheets.
If the destination of a man, who leaves his unit, is known (e.g. on transfer to another unit), his Field Conduct Sheet should be sent by the Officer Commanding his unit to the Officer Commanding the unit at his destination. But if the destination is not definitely known (e.g. in the case of a man sick or wounded), the Field Conduct Sheet will be sent to the A.G's Office at the Base.
(G.R.O. 1154).

631. **WAR DIARIES.**
General Routine Order No. 543 of 14th January, is republished for information, as great inconvenience is caused by the instructions contained therein being disregarded.
"As frequent cases have occurred of War Diaries being received without any covering letter, signature of Officer Commanding Unit, or any other means of identification thereon, attention is called to Field Service Regulations Part II, para 140 (4) which must be strictly adhered to in future."(G.R.O.1155).

632. **IMPROPER DISPOSAL OF RATIONS AND FORAGE.**
The following extract from Army Order 346/1915 is published for information:-
"Cases having occurred of the illicit disposal of rations and forage, it is notified that, in so far as civilians are concerned, such articles remain the property of the State until consumed.
Commanding Officers will take effective measures to ensure that no portion of the ration which is capable of being used as human food is illegally sold or otherwise made away with. They will deal severely with soldiers under their command found to be implicated in such illicit traffic". (G.R.O. 1156).

633. **ENGINEER PAY-TUNNELLING COMPANIES.**
Officers of other arms than Royal Engineers appointed to Tunnelling Companies,Royal Engineers, are entitled to Engineer Pay under precisely the same conditions as Officers of the Royal Engineers.
They will accordingly be eligible for the higher rate of Engineer pay under the conditions laid down in Army Order 333/14.
(Authority War Office Letter No.9/A.S.C./2110 (F.2)dated 13.Sept.1915).
(G.R.O.1157).

634. **FIELD ALLOWANCE-Warrant Officers on Indian rates of Pay.**
The Army Council has authorised the issue of Field Allowance (under the same conditions as laid down for Warrant Officers of units on British Pay)to Warrant Officers (Classes I & II)of British Units serving with the Indian Expeditionary Force in France,and also to Warrant Officers of British units sent from India but not forming part of that Force. In the case of Warrant Officers ClassI the daily allowance of 1/- will be admissible from the date of embarkation for active service,or from the date of appointment,if later.
In the case of Warrant Officers Class II the daily allowance of 6d will not be admissible prior to the date of the creation of that rank i.e.the 28th January 1915. (Authority W.O.letter 121/Finance/350 (Q.M.G. F.a) dated 21st August 1915. (G.R.O.1159).

P. T. O.

635. **SNIPERSCOPES.**
Approval is given for the issue of "Espitallier Sniperscopes" on a scale of 8 per Battalion. Indents should be sent to Ordnance Officers concerned, and issue will be made as supplies become available. (G.R.O. 1161).

636. **MINCING MACHINES.**
Approval is given for the issue of Mincing Machines to Infantry Battalions on a scale of one per Company. Indents should be sent to Ordnance Officers concerned and issue will be made as supplies become available. (G.R.O. 1162).

637. **CLINOMETERS.**
Approval is given for the issue of two additional clinometers per Regular Infantry Battalion to allow of one being used for each machine gun. These, if not already demanded, should be indented for through the usual channel, and supply will be made as they become available. (G.R.O. 1163).

638. **MAIL BAGS - IRREGULAR USE OF.**
It has been brought to notice that empty mail bags are often used by units for sending old stores to the Base and other irregular purposes, instead of returning them to the Army Postal Service at the earliest opportunity.
Unless the prompt return of all mail bags is ensured the efficiency of the Postal Service will be affected, and certain postal facilities may have to be withdrawn.
Officers Commanding Units will be held responsible that Mail Bags are returned to the Army Postal Service with the least possible delay, and that they are on no account used for other purposes than for that of carrying mails. (G.R.O. 1164.).

639. **RIFLE BREECH COVERS.**
A universal pattern of rifle breech cover has been introduced, suitable for either long, short or Ross rifle.
Indents may be submitted on the scale of one per rifle, and supply will be made as they become available.
Local provision of rifle covers under the terms of General Routine Order No.581, may, however, still be made if preferred. (G.R.O. 1165).

640. **LEAVE**
Only urgent cases for leave will at present be considered.

641. **BATHING.**
No bathing in the Canal is allowed between CAPPY Bridge and the lock at FROISSY.

642. **SALVAGE COMPANY.**
The Officer N.C.Os and men of this Company together with the hand carts will report to the A.D.M.S. at MERICOURT at 12 noon on Friday 24th.

643. **PERMANENT COMMISSIONS.**
Reference 27th Division Circular Memorandum 2610 of 14th. September, the 3rd para should read 17 of each month and not 20th as stated.

644. **PROMOTION OF OFFICERS HOLDING TEMPORARY COMMISSIONS.**
Reference M.S./3730 of 18th August, recommendations for such promotion should reach this Office by the 23rd of each month.

644. **PASSAGES FROM ABROAD.**
With reference to Army Order 300 of August 1915, all claims for payment of refund for cost of passage from abroad, will be submitted, through the usual channels to the War Office for decision. The following cases are however not entitled to refunds and should be so decided without reference to this Office:-
Civilians, Time Expired Reservists, and men with previous service who were discharged with the rank of Private, and who proceeded to United Kingdom to enlist entirely upon their own initiative.
Also Civilians without previous Military Service who came from abroad to the United Kingdom, entirely upon their own initiative, and obtained commissions, are similarly not entitled.
(H.Q. 3rd Army Q.C./783, 27th Division 2632/1).

645. **AMMUNITION**
In all cases where ammunition is found to be faulty, some of a like nature is to be retained for examination purposes.
The specimens should be forwarded, with reports concerning same to this Office.(3rd Army Q.C./713, 27th Div. 0/719.).

646. **SOLUTION FOR SPRAYING.**
Solution for spraying smoke helmets will be drawn as follows:-

Infantry Units - From the Field Ambulance affiliated to their Brigade.
All other Units, from the nearest Field Ambulance.

647. **REFILLING**.
Refilling on morning of 25th. will be as follows:-
80th Brigade Formation) MERICOURT - 9 a.m.
82nd Brigade Formation)

Divisional Troops, MORCOURT 9 a.m.

81st Brigade Formation - CERISY GAILLY 9 a.m.

H.J. EVERETT, Colonel.

A.A. and Q.M.G., 27th. Division.

AFTER ORDER.

648. **NOMINAL ROLLS - OFFICERS.**
Nominal rolls of Officers by units are to be rendered to this Office, through the usual channels by 6 p.m. 26th. instant. These rolls are to be made up to 12 noon tomorrow, showing opposite their names, whether regular, Special Reserve, Territorial or Temporary Commissioned, and the name of the unit, to which any officers who are attached belong.

DIVISIONAL ROUTINE ORDERS, No. 112.

by

MAJOR GENERAL G.F. MILNE, C.B., D.S.O., Commanding 27th Division.

25th September 1915.

649. TRENCH ORDERS.
The attention of all ranks is called to 3rd Army Trench Orders issued today.

650. TRAFFIC CONTROL.
(a) All orders affecting traffic control issued by Brigade Commanders are to be submitted to Divisional Headquarters for approval before issue. The Motor Car of the G.O.C. the Division is not to be stopped by any sentry.

(b) The road running along the South bank of the canal between CAPPY and FROISSY is available only for mounted Officers, dismounted troops and cyclists. Traffic will be allowed both ways. No vehicles except Divisional Motor Cars are allowed to use this road.
The orders for sentries are to be altered accordingly.

(c) Special instructions for traffic in case of an emergency are being issued to all concerned.

651. SANITATION.
It is noticed that units are neglecting the sanitary regulations necessary for the good health of the troops. Incinerators and properly constructed latrines are to be commenced at once.
Medical Officers will consult with Commanding Officers as regards safeguarding the drinking water supply which should be marked and protected against any contamination.
Notice boards for drinking water places, washing and bathing, to be put up.
Attention is called to the necessity of chlorinating all water used for drinking purposes.

652. POSTAL SERVICES.
On and after Monday 27th instant, Postal Refilling Point for all units will be at MERICOURT.

653. DESPATCH OF DETAILS TO BASE &c.
Attention is called to Circular Memorandum No. A/2539 issued with Divisional Routine Order No. 525 dated 30th August 1915, on the subject of the Despatch of Details to the BASE etc. Much correspondence would be avoided if the instructions contained therein were carried out. Serious notice will be taken of any neglect to do so in future.

H.J. EVERETT.   Colonel.
A.A. and Q.M.G.,   27th. Division

Map References 27th Divn. Aid Posts etc
Sheet 36. 1/20,000

19th Field Ambulance	H 4 d	4.7		
81st do do	H 3 d	9.2		Dressing
83rd do do	B 30 d	3.5		Stations
82nd do do	B 30 d	6.6		

19th Field Ambulance	H 24 b	1.9	
81st do do	I 1 d	6.5	
83rd do do	C 26 b	9.2	Advanced
82nd do do	C 21 b	4.1 ※	D.S.

19th Brigade	1	H 20 b	5.8	
19th Fd Amb.	2	I 19 b	0.3	
	3	I 19 a	9.8	R.A.P.
	T	I 25 a	9.1 ※	

81st Brigade   1 I 14 d 3.9
81st Fd Amb.   2 I 15 c 2.8 ※
                3 I 15 b 3.6 ※

80th Brigade   1 I 9 a b 0.4
83rd Fd Amb.   2 C 28 a 1.1 ※
                T I 4 b   2.5 ※

82nd Brigade   1⎫
82nd Fd Amb.   2⎬ C 21 d 9.9
                3⎬
                4⎭ C 22 a 3.6

        A I 1 c 3.5 ※   R.A.P.
        B I 1 d 5.7   R.F.A.
        C C 26 b   ※

121/7498

A.D.M.S. 27th Div.

Dec '15

Vol X

Oct 1915

WAR DIARY
or
INTELLIGENCE SUMMARY

Army Form C. 2118

(Erase heading not required.)

Instructions regarding War Diaries and Intelligence Summaries are contained in F. S. Regs., Part II. and the Staff Manual respectively. Title pages will be prepared in manuscript.

Place	Date	Hour	Summary of Events and Information	Remarks and references to Appendices
MERICOURT	1/4/15	—	Sick officers 3 O.R. 21. wounded " — " — 6.	G.F. Ruston Captain Veterinary Officer
			Divisional order published as to arrangements for carrying the W.O. to be adapted to meet times for Routine order re Service feet. Rame.	
	2/4/15	—	Sick officers 1 O.R. 45. wounded " — O.R. 10. Slave Brigade Mining Sections known such known of respective Brigade areas. When employed in line they will obtain medical aid from nearest Regimental Aid Post. O.C. Sections have been informed as to location of Aid Post on front area — where an ample supply of oxygen is available.	I
	3/4/15	"	Sick officers nil O.R. 26. wounded " — 1	[stamp: A.D.M.S. 27th DIVISION]

2353 Wt. W3541/1454 700,000 5/15 D.D.&L. A.D.S.S./Form/C. 2118.

WAR DIARY or INTELLIGENCE SUMMARY

Army Form C. 2118

(Erase heading not required.)

Instructions regarding War Diaries and Intelligence Summaries are contained in F. S. Regs., Part II and the Staff Manual respectively. Title pages will be prepared in manuscript.

Place	Date	Hour	Summary of Events and Information	Remarks and references to Appendices
MERICOURT	4/4/15		Sick officers nil 2 O.R. 30. wounded — 2. O.R. 8. Stat. Field Ambulance take over Advanced Dressing Station at CHUIGNES from 3rd Field Amb — in charge of respective Brigades. Divisions pushed attacking Batt home.	II
"	5/4/15		Sick officers nil O.R. 24. wounded — 1 O.R. 4 Inspected Regimental Aid Posts of 2nd Elshires and Royal Scots at FONTAINE LES CAPPY. Divisional order issued re issue of antifebrine & precautions to avoid wearing dress — also as to further precautions to be taken by units in prevention of trench feet.	III
"	6/4/15		Sick officers 1 O.R. 39 wounded — — O.R. 3.	

WAR DIARY
or
INTELLIGENCE SUMMARY.
(Erase heading not required.)

Army Form C. 2118

Place	Date	Hour	Summary of Events and Information	Remarks and references to Appendices
MERICOURT	7/10/15	—	Sick officers 2 O.R. 70. Wounded — nil — 2. DMS 2nd Army inspected Barg's no and 82nd Field Ambulance at LANEUVILLE	
"	8/10/15		Sick officers 3 O.R. 22. Wounded — nil — 1. Arrangement made with S.S.O. to be drawn from the Division, as employed over land being handed over to Field Ambulances for preparation of anticipated scheme.	
"	9/10/15		Sick officers 1 O.R. 17. Wounded " nil " 4. DDMS 17th Corps inspected Barg's no and Dressing Station of 82nd Field Ambulance.	
"	10/10/15		Sick officers 1 O.R. 30. Wounded " nil " nil	

Army Form C. 2118

WAR DIARY
or
INTELLIGENCE SUMMARY.
(Erase heading not required.)

Instructions regarding War Diaries and Intelligence Summaries are contained in F. S. Regs., Part II. and the Staff Manual respectively. Title pages will be prepared in manuscript.

Place	Date	Hour	Summary of Events and Information	Remarks and references to Appendices
MERICOURT	11/10/15		Sick officers 3. O.R. 9. wounded — nil O.R. 6. Various all ranks Ambulances	
"	12/10/15		Sick officers nil O.R. 19. wounded — 1 O.R. 3	
"	13/10/15		Sick officers nil O.R. 15 wounded nil O.R. 4. 82nd Inf. Brigade temporarily detailed from the Divn. and attached to 22nd Division. The Field Ambulance (83rd) appointed to the Brigade will not accompany them. The 67th Inf. Bde 22nd Divn. temporarily join the Divn. in relief and become Divisional Reserve.	
"	14/10/15		Sick officers nil O.R. 11 wounded — nil O.R. 4 Divisional Order published re water supply. Pointed out G. "Q" the General deficiency and condition of various wells in our area. Ramy of the well see Memorandum Statement, an account of Borehole work etc.	IV

G.W. Ricks Captain

Army Form C. 2118

WAR DIARY
or
INTELLIGENCE SUMMARY.
(Erase heading not required.)

Place	Date	Hour	Summary of Events and Information	Remarks and references to Appendices
MERICOURT	15/10/15		Sick officers 2. O.R. nil. Wounded — " " nil O.R. 2. Selected a house in ABANCOURT as an Officers Convalescent Depot for the Divn. a very suitable building, but much furniture is required to make it satisfactory. O.C. 8th Fld. Amb. instructed to take it over with a view to opening it as soon as possible.	
"	16/10/15		Sick officers nil O.R. 16 Wounded — " nil O.R. 2	
"	17/10/15		Sick officers nil O.R. 11 Wounded — " 1 O.R. nil. 67th Inf. Brigade relieve 80th Brigade in trenches left sector. 2nd Field Ambulance takes over Advanced Dressing Station at CAPPY to collect sick and wounded of 67th Brigade. 80th Brigade became Divisional Reserve. Arrangements made for the dentist to attend sick cases at the Divisional Rest Station every Wednesday.	[signature] Captain

WAR DIARY
or
INTELLIGENCE SUMMARY.
(Erase heading not required.)

Army Form C. 211

Place	Date	Hour	Summary of Events and Information	Remarks and references to Appendices
MERICOURT	19/10/15		Sick officers 2 O.R. 31. wounded — nil O.R. 5. Visited 183 Tunnelling Coy R.E. engaged winning operations at FONTAINE les CAPPY. December with a view to arranging details re medical assistance and supply of oxygen cylinders in case of "gassing" accident, each O.C. is supplied with 13 Reviving apparatuses and 1 N.C.O. & 4 men from each Section have been instructed in their use. Oxygen Cylinders and bags, two to each Company above be provided and placed under charge of each O.C. Company. The Corps have been asked to make the issue.	
"	19/10/15		Sick officers nil O.R. 50 wounded — nil O.R. 2	
"	20/10/15		Sick officers 2 O.R. 13 wounded — nil O.R. 4 All leave stopped and Unit warned to prepare to move.	

WAR DIARY
INTELLIGENCE SUMMARY
(Erase heading not required.)

Army Form C. 2118

Instructions regarding War Diaries and Intelligence Summaries are contained in F. S. Regs., Part II. and the Staff Manual respectively. Title pages will be prepared in manuscript.

Place	Date	Hour	Summary of Events and Information	Remarks and references to Appendices
MERICOURT	21/10/15		Sick officers nil O.R. 14 wounded — nil O.R. 3	
"	22/10/15		Sick officers 1 O.R. 16 wounded — nil O.R. nil. 32nd Fld Amb. relieve 2nd Field Amb. at A.D.M.S. Cappy on account of the 82nd Fd Amb. wanting fresh. Visited all Field Ambulances in preparatory to move. Also visited A.D.M.S. 5th Division to arrange handing over Bargt 140. at FRISE. The 2nd and the Bargs will be handed over on the 23rd and any patient unfit for return to their unit in accompany the Division will remain and Bargt subsequently be sent on or be evacuated.	
"	23/10/15		Sick officers nil O.R. 16 wounded — nil O.R. 3. Leave reopen to all ranks. The 2nd Fd. Amb. move from PROYART to [illegible] in order to render bil[illegible] Cap[illegible] any. WARFUSEE - PERONNE Road in order to PROYART.	

WAR DIARY
or
INTELLIGENCE SUMMARY.

(Erase heading not required.)

Army Form C. 2118

Place	Date	Hour	Summary of Events and Information	Remarks and references to Appendices
MERICOURT	23/10/15 continued		Operation orders received to hand 2nd Amb. re-move stores with 82nd Brigade to BOVES. Capt. G. Cook transferred from 82nd Fd. Amb. as medical officer i/c 1st Leinster Regt. in relief of Capt. R.E. Delgado – evacuated sick. Capt. R.E. Mantrith ordered to report to D.D.M.S. Rouen for duty on 25th inst. Operation orders issued to all units to move. Sick officers ad. off. 78 wounded " " " 1	
"	24/10/15		Revd. 2nd Amb. march to BOVES with 82nd Brigade. Visited Sgt. Fd. Amb. Head Station saw all move on hospital – probably about 30 cases will not move. Sgt. 2d Amb. will leave sufficient personnel behind to look after them and bring them on later.	

WAR DIARY or INTELLIGENCE SUMMARY

Army Form C. 2118

Place	Date	Hour	Summary of Events and Information	Remarks and references to Appendices
MERICOURT	25/10/15		Sick officers 1 O.R. 20 wounded — nil O.R. nil. Capt. R.G. Manterips Rand M.O. to 1 DCLI proceeds to ROUEN to report to D.D.M.S. Lieut. K.F. Lowday posted as medical officer on return. 32nd Fd. Amb. + 80th Bde. march on from BOVES to new area.	
	26/10/15		Sick officers nil O.R. 16 wounded — nil O.R. 2. 81st Fd. Amb. march with 81st Inf. Brigade to BOVES. H.Qn. 27th Div, including A.D.M.S. move to new area about BOVELLES — S.W. AMIENS.	
BOVELLES	27/10/15		Sick officers nil O.R. 28 wounded nil — Division now out of action. 81st Fd. Amb. + 81st Inf. Bde. march on from BOVES to new area. 82nd Fd. Amb. march with 80th Brigade from Trench to BOVES. 82nd Fd. Amb. [...] occupy Billets at FRESNOY — now are [Captain signature]	

WAR DIARY
or
INTELLIGENCE SUMMARY.

(Erase heading not required.)

Army Form C. 2118

Place	Date	Hour	Summary of Events and Information	Remarks and references to Appendices
BOESELEES	28/10/15		Sick officers ord O.R. 75. Std. Fd. Amb. occupy billets at MONTENOY – new area. 80th Brigade & 83rd Fd. Amb. march from BOVES to new area. Arrangements made for evacuation of sick from 82nd & 83rd Brigade areas by respective Fd. Ambulances.	
"	29/10/15		Sick officers at O.R. 3. 82nd Field Ambulance occupy billets at FLUY. Std. Field Ambulance move to billets at BONGAINVILLE. Arrangements made for collection of sick at 80th Brigade area.	
"	30/10/15		Sick officers 3 O.R. 17. A.D.M.S. inspects units of all infantry units.	

WAR DIARY or INTELLIGENCE SUMMARY.

Army Form C. 2118

Place	Date	Hour	Summary of Events and Information	Remarks and references to Appendices
BOVELLES			With reference to D.R.O. 3). R.O.M. inspected empts of 80th Brigade at return received — copy of inoculation return attached. Map of Inocl. area same as last month. Composed Division occupied same trenches. Genl. location of units as follows:- Sat. Fd. Amb. BOUGAINVILLE 82nd " FRESNOY 83rd " FLUY. Sanitary Section BOVELLES Workshop Unit FLUY. One Section of No. X M.A.C. at FLUY. 1 Case of Influenza during month 1 Case of Trench Spinal fever " 1 Case of Mumps " J.A. Rushin Captain for A.D.M.S. (Absent on leave)	V

DIVISIONAL ROUTINE ORDERS, No. 117.

by

MAJOR GENERAL G.F. MILNE, C.B., D.S.O., Commanding 27th Division.

1st October 1915.

690. REFILLING.

On and after October 2nd refilling will take place at 4 p.m. at the following places:-

Divisional Troops Formation. .... MORCOURT.

80th Brigade Formation. .... MERICOURT.

81st) Brigade Formations .... CERISY-GAILLY.
82nd)

Supply Wagons of the Train after refilling will park for the night with the Train Company to which they belong and on the following morning will proceed to the billets of the units and dump supplies.

691. INTERPRETERS.

1. Owing to the reduced numbers now with the Division, Interpreters can no longer be considered as the exclusive property of the unit with which they happen to be billeted. They will be for use with any group of units which the Liaison Officer may order from time to time.

2. Interpreters are not to go or to be sent on commissions by Officers outside the Divisional Area without permission from the Liaison Officer.

692. LAUNDRIES.

Arrangements have been made for the laundry work of the Division to be carried out at BOVES- The following instructions must be carefully adhered to, to ensure the satisfactory working of the scheme:-

(1) Soiled clothes will be collected at the various baths of the Division, placed in sacks, packed very loosely, (vests, shirts, drawers and socks packed separately) these should be labelled showing numbers of contents.

(2) The sacks will then be despatched by O.C. Baths in a G.S. Wagon so as to reach the baths at MERICOURT not later than 10 a.m. every Sunday, Tuesday and Thursday.

(3) Clean clothes will be issued from the Baths, MERICOURT on the same day in return for the soiled clothes delivered. No clean clothes, however, can be given out in exchange for the 1st lot of soiled sent in - it being presumed that men are already provided with one change of clothing.

The scheme will come into operation on Sunday next the 3rd prox.

693. ORDERS.

Many instances have come to notice of men being unacquainted with orders. The G.O.C directs that all orders which immediately affect the men are to be read out 3 times on parade. When units are in the trenches those orders are to be read out when they come into reserve.

694. DISCIPLINE.

Troops are forbidden to make use of the civilian latrines in their billets - other latrine accommodation must be provided by units.

P.T.O.

695. OIL AND CRESOL DRUMS.
All empty oil and cresol drums will be handed over to 27th. Divisional Sanitary Section at their headquarters, MERICOURT, or at detachments of the Section located in LANEUVILLE-MORCOURT, PROYART and WARFUSEE.

696. BILLETS.
All billets West and exclusive of the line CAPPY-CHUIGNES-HERLEVILLE will be paid for. Any substantial billets East of this line, which in the opinion of the O.C.Unit concerned are deserving of payment will also be paid for.

697. TRENCH FEET.
With the approach of cold weather all ranks should be warned as to methods of preventing "chilled feet". A preparation for application to feet of trench troops will shortly be available.
It is most important that particular attention is paid to the proper fitting of boots, which should be loosely laced and sufficiently large enough for two pairs of socks to be worn.
Boots and socks should be removed as often as circumstances permit but at least once a day and the feet warmed by rubbing them, never at a fire. Paper wrapped round the feet, either on the inside or outside of sock, will prevent cold feet but requires to be changed immediately it gets damp.
On leaving the trenches regimental arrangements should be made when possible to provide clean and dry towels, cold water and soap, for the purpose of thoroughly washing and drying the feet, after which dry socks should be put on. Hot water must on no account be used for this purpose. Puttees should never be put on tightly.

698. BURIAL GROUNDS.
Reference Circular Memorandum No.1575/2 of 9th September, para 6 will be amended to read:-
Left Infantry Brigade...(a) Orchard 1000 metres East of CAPPY on DOMPIERRE Road.
(b) East of Canal Lock at ECLUSIER
(c) 1000 metres North of CAPPY(Cemetery).

Right Infantry Brigade..(a) Extension of French Military Cemetery on North of Church at Fontaine des CAPPY.
(b) Cemetery about 1500 metres along the Fontaine des CAPPY-FONCAUCOURT Road.

Reserve Brigade, Divisional Troops - Further instructions will be issued.

699. DISCIPLINE.
The Commander-in-Chief regrets to notice a prevalence of the most serious and dangerous offence of "Sleeping on the Post".
It has not been necessary up to the present time to carry out the extreme penalty in relation to this offence, but the number of cases which have recently occurred have caused the Commander-in-Chief to decide that he will have no alternative but to carry out the extreme penalty in the future. This order is to be read out on Parade three times. (G.R.O. 1168).

700. BOMBS AND GRENADES.
In order to avoid confusion Chemical Bombs will in future be called "BOMBS" and high explosive bombs "GRENADES".

DIVISIONAL ROUTINE ORDERS, No. 120.

by

MAJOR GENERAL G.F. MILNE, C.B., D.S.O., Commanding 27th Division.

4th October, 1915.

718. **TUNNELLING COMPANIES, R.E.**
All Officers and men posted to Tunnelling Companies can be replaced by drafts (if available) from the Base, but they are not to be struck off the strength of their unit till their transfer is completed, i.e. not until a notification has been received from R.E. Records that a regimental number has been allotted (Authority D.A.G., Base C.R. No.3812, dated 14-9-15).

All men employed assisting in tunnelling operations, other than men belonging to Tunnelling Companies, must not be struck off the strength of units, but drafts (if available) may be demanded from the Base by entering the numbers so employed on the back of the perforated sheet attached to A.F. B 213 as "Employed assisting Tunnelling Companies". (Authority A.G., G.H.Q., dated 13-9-1915). (Extract from A.R.O.76)

719. **COURTS MARTIAL.**
Captain Cockerell, 3rd Army, will be available for the 12th Corps area on Wednesdays and Saturdays in each week as fourth member of a Court Martial in Cases of Desertion, Cowardice and in complicated cases. If this Officer's services are required by Convening Officers notice by wire should be given to Divisional Headquarters at least 38 hours in advance, giving time and place of assembly of the Court.

720. **WATERING OF HORSES.**
Horses will not be watered from the canal west of the lock at FROISSY but in the ponds East of the Y in LANEUVILLE LES BRAY.

721. **OLD HORSE SHOES-DISPOSAL OF.**
Old horse shoes which cannot be used for the manufacture of new shoes should be returned to Railheads for transmission to the Base. They should be packed whenever possible, in empty horse shoe boxes. (G.R.O. 1179).

722. **TORCHES ELECTRIC.**
A statement showing the number of electric torches held by units and Heads of Departments, and quoting authority under which held, if possible, will be sent to D.A.D.O.S. by 12 noon on Tuesday 5th instant. (12th Corps wire Q/424 - 27th.Division 0/765).

723. **RIFLE MUZZLE PROTECTORS.**
Rifle muzzle protectors can be indented for when required, under authority D.O.S., O.S.B./1098 dated 27-9-15.
A new pattern protector (Howell Pattern) is being supplied, but if not available, and urgently required, No 2 pattern will be issued in lieu. (O//43/12, 27th.Division 0/764).

724. **REVISED A.F. B.213.**
The attention of all concerned is directed to General Routine Order No 1175 dated 27th Ultimo, especially to the instructions as to compilation of Army Form B.213 dealing with the Effective Strength of unit and attached Officers and men.

P.T.O.

725. PASSES.
Reference Divisional Routine Order No.654 of 26th September, all civilian passes will in future be signed by the A.P.M. only.
All passes presented to units will be forwarded to him by Despatch Rider.

726. HIRE OF LAND.
Agreements will be made for all grass land used as wagon and horse lines. In the area now occupied, not more than two francs per acre should be paid, and this sum should cover a period of 12 months.

727. REINFORCEMENTS.
Reference Circular Memorandum 2642 of 24th September, paras 5,6 and 7 are cancelled and the following will be substituted:-

Advice. (5) Units will be warned as early as possible of the arrival of drafts or details over 10 strong.

(6) The Staff of the Rest Camp will be responsible for guiding drafts or details from the Rest Camp as follows:-
    (a) In the case of Infantry, to units or Brigade Hd.Qrs. if in any doubt.
    (b) .. .. R.A. to the Divisional Ammunition Column, HAMEL

Disposal
    (c) .. .. R. E. to C.R.E., MERICOURT.
    (d) ,, ... R.A.M.C. to 81st Field Ambulance, MORCOURT.
    (e) .. .. A. S. C. to Train Headquarters, MORCOURT.

Kits. (7) Officers' and other kits will have to be sent for to Railhead.

728. BATHS.
The following is the allotment of the baths in the Divisional Area:-

CAPPY Baths. Worked under arrangements made by O.C. 83rd Field Ambulance. For all troops situated in the Left Brigade area. To be allotted by G.O.C., Brigade holding left Sector.

PROYART Baths. Worked under arrangements made by O.C. 82nd Field Ambulance. For all troops situated in the Right Brigade Area. To be allotted by G.O.C., Brigade holding right sector.

MORCOURT Baths. Worked under arrangements made by O.C. 81st Field Ambulance. For all troops situated in the Reserve Area, except one battalion, which will be bathed at MERICOURT. To be allotted by G.O.C. Brigade in reserve.

MERICOURT Baths. Worked and allotted under arrangements made by Divisional Headquarters,
Mondays. Morning-Divisional Hd.Qrs. Afternoon, R.A.Units.
Tuesday. 300 men of Brigade in Reserve.
Wednesday. Morning, Divl.Yeomanry-Afternoon, R.A. Units.
Thursday. 300 men of Brigade in Reserve.
Friday. Morning, Divl.Cyclist Co.-Afternoon, R.A. Units.
Saturdays. 300 men of Brigade in Reserve.

H.J. EVERETT, Colonel,
A.A. and Q.M.G. 27th Division.

DIVISIONAL ROUTINE ORDERS, No. 729.

by

MAJOR GENERAL G.F. MILNE, C.B., D.S.O., Commanding 27th, Division.

5th October, 1915.

729. **TRENCH FEET.**

In continuation of Divisional Routine Order No.697 of the 1st instant, units will draw Anti-frostbite grease (Special Preparation) from the Field Ambulance affiliated to their Brigade, as supplies become available. The supply of the preparation is at present limited and only units actually in the trenches should apply for the same.

Instructions regarding the use of this ointment are as follows:-

(1) Immediately before troops proceed to the trenches, puttees, boots and socks should be removed, the feet and legs as far as the knees will be washed with cold water and thoroughly dried, the ointment should then be applied to the whole surface of the skin from the knees down and especially between the toes. Good serviceable socks should then be put on, the boots loosely laced and puttees loosely adjusted.

(2) This procedure with the omission of washing will be gone through when possible every 24 hours the troops remain in the trenches.

(3) On return to billets care must be taken that hot water is not used to bathe the feet for at least 48 hours afterwards.

(4) It is of the utmost importance that every man going to the trenches shall be in possession of 2 pairs of socks in good condition, in addition to the pair he is wearing, he should also carry a towel with which to dry his feet and legs when he removes his boots.

730. **IRON RATIONS.**

Iron rations have now been made up. In future any unit requiring iron rations will forward through the usual channels to Divisional Headquarters an indent in duplicate, together with a certificate or statement showing clearly the reason for the requirement.

731. **SOYER'S STOVES.**

Soyer's Stoves have been allotted to units. They will be considered as trench or area stores and not moved when units move from one place to another. It is suggested that those stoves allotted to battalions in the trenches should be used for making tea etc,. for the troops in the trenches.

H.J. EVERETT,   Colonel.
A.A. and Q.M.G., 27th Division.

DIVISIONAL ROUTINE ORDERS, No. 130.

by

MAJOR GENERAL G.F. MILNE, C.B., D.S.O., Commanding 27th Division.

14th October 1915.

791. WATER SUPPLY.
It has been brought to notice that the deep wells in PROYART and Warfusee-Abancourt, are gradually being put out of use owing the reels, ropes &c being broken due entirely to the fact that water drawing parties allow the bucket to run down into the well of its own accord instead of being lowered gradually,

In future the unit, in whose billeting area the well is situated, will be responsible for the upkeep of the plant and the drawing of water. A water drawing party is to be detailed daily whose duty it will be to fill water carts etc.

Water is only to be drawn at stated hours to be fixed by the Infantry Brigadier in whose area the well is. The requirements of the inhabitants must be considered.

Reels will be repaired by the Battalion Pioneers. Buckets and rope can be obtained from the D.A.D.O.S.

Owing to the high ground surrounding the village of CHUIGNOLLES, there is serious risk of the water supply being fouled after heavy rains. Units occupying billets are to be warned and water discipline strictly enforced..

792. DISCIPLINE.
In accordance with para 583 King's Regulations, it is notified for information that the crime of "Sleeping on Post" is unusually prevalent in the Division. The G.O.C. directs that Section 6.1.(K) of the Army Act be read out three times to the men on parade. Commanding Officers will so arrange parades that every man in their unit shall be present at one time or the other when this Section is read out.

793. DIVINE SERVICE. - Church of England.
(1) Brigade Chaplains will arrange with Commanding Officers for Parade Services, when possible, for units of their Brigade and for certain Divisional Units billeted in their area, and will communicate to all concerned the times and places of such Parade Services.

(2) Remainder of Divisional Troops.

8-45 a.m. Parade Service. - Place - Chateau Grounds.
          Hd.Qrs.
          Troops. All within radius of one mile.

10-45 a.m. Parade Service.- Place, CERISY, 97th Coy.A.S.C.,lines.
           Troops, all in or near CERISY.

11-45 a.m. Parade Service.
           Place - Billets of 2nd Section, 27th. Divl.Ammn.Col.
           Troops - 27th Divisional Ammunition Column.

5 p.m.   Parade Service. - Place, HAMELET
          Troops. - 27th Divl.Supply Column. 27th Reserve Park
                    21st Reserve Park.

H.J. EVERETT. Colonel.

A.A. and Q.M.G. 27th Division.

MONTHLY INOCULATION RETURN.

27th Division.   Month ending 31st October 1915.

Unit.	Strength Offrs.	Strength O.Rks.	Inoculated Offrs.	Inoculated O.Ranks.	Percentage Offrs.	Percentage O.Rks.	Numbers inoculated during mth.
H.Q. Unit 27th Divn.	14	70	14	70	100.	100.	-
2nd K.Shropshire L.I.	25	951	25	951	100.	100.	-
3rd K.R.R.Corps.	24	932	22	932	91.7	100.	3
4th K.R.R.Corps.	26	950	26	950	100.	100.	-
4th Rifle Brigade.	26	964	25	941	96.2	97.6	-
P.P.Canadian L.I.	31	966	31	959	100.	99.3	1
1st Royal Scots.	24	840	24	833	100.	99.2	-
2nd Gloster Regt.	28	1028	22	936	78.6	91.	-
2nd Cameron Hldrs.	29	993	29	993	100.	100.	-
1st A.& S.Hldrs.	25	1039	25	1034	100.	99.5	-
9th Royal Scots.	30	765	30	765	100.	100.	-
1st R.Irish Regt.	28	854	28	834	100.	97.6	-
2nd D.C.L.Inf.	22	933	20	928	90.9	99.4	-
2nd R.Irish Fus.	26	894	26	894	100.	100.	-
1st Leinster Regt.	27	855	27	855	100.	100.	-
1st Cambs.Regt.	31	857	31	851	100.	99.3	-
H.Qrs.R.A.	4	20	4	20	100.	100.	-
1st Brigade R.F.A.	26	775	26	774	100.	99.8	-
19th do do	21	745	21	736	100.	98.8	9
20th do do	27	760	27	736	100.	96.8	-
129th do do	18	498	18	492	100.	98.8	-
27th Div.Ammn.Col.R.F.A.	15	505	13	492	86.6	97.4	-
27th Div.Engineers.	21	625	21	613	100.	98.	4
27th Div.Train A.S.C.	25	424	25	391	100.	92.2	3
27th Div.Cyclists.	9	196	9	196	100.	100.	-
27th Div.Signal Coy.R.E.	9	232	9	232	100.	100.	-
----do----Cable Section.	1	34	1	34	100.	100.	-
27th Div.Yeomanry.	6	138	6	137	100.	99.2	-
16th Mobile Vet.Section.	1	26	1	26	100.	100.	-
27th Div.Sanitary Sec.	1	25	1	25	100.	100.	-
81st Field Ambulance.	10	238	10	238	100.	100.	-
82nd Field Ambulance.	8	228	8	226	100.	99.1	-
83rd Field Ambulance.	10	240	10	231	100.	96.2	-
27th F.A.Workshops.	1	19	1	19	100.	100.	-
Total	629.	19,619	616.	19,344.	97.9.	98.6.	20.

H.Q. 27th Div.

31st October 1915.

Colonel A.M.S.,

A.D.M.S., 27th Division.

A.D.M.S. 27th Div.

Nov.
Vol XI

12/751

Nov 1915

Army Form C. 2118

WAR DIARY
or
INTELLIGENCE SUMMARY.
(Erase heading not required.)

Instructions regarding War Diaries and Intelligence Summaries are contained in F. S. Regs., Part II. and the Staff Manual respectively. Title pages will be prepared in manuscript.

Place	Date	Hour	Summary of Events and Information	Remarks and references to Appendices
BOVELLES	4-11-15	—	Sick officers nil other ranks 33. A.D.M.S. inspected unfits of all Brigades with a view to weeding out "old men" unable to march etc. for transfer to the base until fit for service at the front.	SMR
		2.11.15	Sick officers 2 other ranks 37. Smoke helmets, all avail., withdrawn for known defect.	SMR
		3.11.15	Sick officers 1 other ranks 16. All artillery Units inspected for unfits.	SMR
		4.11.15	Sick officers nil other ranks 34. Heavy Draught Horses withdrawn from Field Ambulances in exchange for mules. Capt. J.A. Smith & Lieut. D.W. McAdam ordered to join Field Ambulance for duty.	

J.A. Rushton Captain
D.A.D.M.S. 27 Div.

Army Form C. 2118

WAR DIARY
or
INTELLIGENCE SUMMARY.
(Erase heading not required.)

Instructions regarding War Diaries and Intelligence Summaries are contained in F.S. Regs., Part II. and the Staff Manual respectively. Title pages will be prepared in manuscript.

[Stamp: A.D.M.S. 27th DIVISION No. ... Date ...]

Place	Date	Hour	Summary of Events and Information	Remarks and references to Appendices
BOVELLES	5/11/15	—	Sick officers nil other ranks 37. One section of No. X Motor Ambulance placed at disposal of A.D.M.S. Billets at FLOY. A.D.M.S. proceeds on leave to England for five days	GWR
	6/11/15	—	Sick officers nil other ranks 18.	GWR
	7/11/15	—	Sick officers nil other ranks 18. Visited all Field Ambulances & arrangements for embarkation of Field Amb. according to Embarkation Returns of Fd.Amb. according to SALONIKA Establishment. Various odd men of all units employed as useful for service at the front. To date 307 men have been sent to the Base as unfit. D.D.M.S. L. of C. to H.Q. Division.	GWR
	8/11/15		Sick officers' other ranks 19. Capt. C.A. Wilson arrives & posted to Fd. Amb.	

W.Rushen Captain
D.A.D.M.S 27th

WAR DIARY
or
INTELLIGENCE SUMMARY
(Erase heading not required.)

Army Form C. 2118

Place	Date	Hour	Summary of Events and Information	Remarks and references to Appendices
BOVELLES	9/11/15	—	Sick officers no other ranks S.S. Laundry at Boves closed. Capt. St. J. D. Burton and Capt. H.D. Clements Smith arrive and posted to 82nd & 83rd Fld Ambs respectively.	GWR
	10/11/15	—	Sick officers nil o.R. 6. Capt. Wm Cash 82nd Fld. Amb. to 1st Div. Capt. J.J. Wagner moved from 1st Cands Regt. to 1st Remlin. Capt. W.D. Anderson from 5th Dn train to 82nd Fld. Amb. Lieut. C.A. Alabaster from 19th Fd.St. R.S.A. to 5th Div. Train. Capt. G. Cook from 82nd Fld. Amb. to 1st Cands Regt. Capt. L.A. Smith from 2nd Fld Amb. to 19th F.D. to R.S.A. R.O.M.S. returns from leave.	SWR
	11/11/15	—	Sick officers nil O.R. 16. Visited all Field Ambulances and inspected transport.	SWR

W.R. Rusher Captain
D.A.D.M.S 27AS

Army Form C. 21

WAR DIARY
or
INTELLIGENCE SUMMARY.
(Erase heading not required.)

Instructions regarding War Diaries and Intelligence Summaries are contained in F.S. Regs., Part II. and the Staff Manual respectively. Title pages will be prepared in manuscript.

Place	Date	Hour	Summary of Events and Information	Remarks and references to Appendices
BOYELLES	10/11/15	—	Sick officers nil O.R. 5. Hazed Ambulance down to complete sick Ambulance 10 each.	Mc
	13/11/15	—	Sick officers 2. O.R. 22. Friction between Chaplain and O.C. 82nd Fd Amb amicably settled by A.D.M.S. Transport officer joins up with Field Ambulance from 5yt Rev Dsn. 1 Case measles in 1st R.S. Regt.	ME
	14/11/15	—	Sick officers 1 O.R. 11. Total unfit to date 361 — certified by A.D.M.S. as unfit for service at the front. Have been all been sent to the Base by Units concerned.	GW
	15/11/15	—	Sick officers nil O.R. 8. 1st Cambs. Regt. to 37th Divn. 2 cases measles in 1st R Lnich. Regt.	M.A.Sh. Captain SA 8 Ind 2/585

2353 Wt. W2544/1454 700,000 5/15 D. D. & L. A.D.S.S./Form/C. 2118.

Army Form C. 2118

WAR DIARY
or
INTELLIGENCE SUMMARY

(Erase heading not required.)

Instructions regarding War Diaries and Intelligence Summaries are contained in F. S. Regs., Part II. and the Staff Manual respectively. Title pages will be prepared in manuscript.

Place	Date	Hour	Summary of Events and Information	Remarks and references to Appendices
BOULZIES	15/11/15 continued	—	1 case of Scarlatina in 19th Bde R.F.A. 80th Brigade commence moving to entrain. All R.M.O. supplied with Vaccine – Antityphoid, Anti Dyspt. Anti Cholera and Camphor for use on voyage.	A.D.M.S. 27th DIVISION
	16/11/15	—	Steep appears nil A.R. 141. Reconnaissance P.A. 6 – 1,000; Daily Slides in and Wounded 7/11 to 3/10/15 – to A.G. Base for safe keeping. R.D.M.S. investigate measles in 1st R.I.R. Heavy Jose of mens. Instructions received for Regimen N.C.O.s Returns to be sent to D.D.M.S. 10th Corps. Enlisted Medical Officers to commence re vaccination as requested in their units.	
	17/11/15		Steep officers nil A.R. 13. All Advance Exchange Book and Coin to be sent to A.G. Base – Note Lg. 23. Blood Log. 8.	SAR

Stewart Capt
DADMS 27 Div

2353 Wt.W3411/1454 750,000 5/15 D.D.&L. ADRS/Forms/C. 2118.

Army Form C. 2118

WAR DIARY
or
INTELLIGENCE SUMMARY.
(Erase heading not required.)

Place	Date	Hour	Summary of Events and Information	Remarks and references to Appendices
BOVERLIES	18.11.15		Sick officers 1 O.R. 19. Another case of measles in 1st R.I. Regt. Another case in 1st R.I.R. all in "D" Coy and in one platoon. The platoon has been segregated and all necessary precautions taken	SMR
	19.11.15		Sick officers nil O.R. 21. Capt. A/D. Anderton from 82nd Fd. Ambulance to 2nd Lieuten. t/o as M.O. Capt. Du Vien from 2nd Cameron H. to 82 F.A.	SMR
	20.11.15		Sick officers 3 O.R. 9. 9th Royal Scots to 5th Division a further case of measles 1st R.S.R. from among contacts of previous cases.	JAR
	21.11.15		Sick officers 1 O.R. 16	

M R Du-- Capt--
A.D.M.S.
27 Div.

WAR DIARY or INTELLIGENCE SUMMARY

Army Form C. 2118

Place: POPERINGHE

Date: 22.11.15

Sick officers > A.R. 43
Capt. Lt. A. Boyd from 80th Fd Amb to 59th Div
Engineers for duty as Medical Officer.
Surg Major E.G. Stocker leaves R.E. encampment N.Y.D.

23.11.15

Sick officers > A.R. 27.
8 Fd. A. & 8 Mac D.S. begin now to station to entrain.
Remnants of members 1st R.I.R. hitched in FERRIERE
on departure of 1st R.I.R.
Capt. R.S.R. Devanaux 82nd Fd. detailed to arrive duties of 19.D. to Transport Section of Old Amb. remaining behind. Temporarily also to supervise conducts daily sick officers at A.R. 6.

24.11.15

All Field Ambulances, Cav Transport entrain. Moto, Ambulance and Moto Cycles handed over to send Ambulance workshop to remain behind.

Camp Marshal of (Lt. Workshop Section) Lieut Newton Kreitmayer

M.M.Sh Capt
D.A.D.M.S

Army Form C. 2118

WAR DIARY
or
INTELLIGENCE SUMMARY.
(Erase heading not required.)

Place	Date	Hour	Summary of Events and Information	Remarks and references to Appendices
BOUELLES	25.11.15		Sick officers nil. O.R. 7. R.A.M.S. (Claims office) proceed to Marseilles. All Infantry are now en route to new area.	
	26.11.15		Sick officers nil. O.R. 5.	
	27.11.15		Sick officers nil. O.R. 5.	
	28.11.15		Sick officers nil. O.R. 3.	
	29.11.15		Sick officers nil. O.R. 2.	
	30.11.15		Sick officers nil. O.R. 3. During the month, 4 cases of measles - all 1st R. Scots. Rgt. One case of Dysentery in 19th Fd. Amb. R.S.a. Enteric Nil. Inoculation Return not forwarded for November, all Units in process of move to new area.	

J.F. Rushin
Lieut.
Lieut. A.D.M.S. 27th Divn.

aw MS 24. Dec
Rec
Vol XII

Fluell

Dec 1915

Army Form C. 2118.

WAR DIARY
or
INTELLIGENCE SUMMARY.
(Erase heading not required.)

A.D.M.S. 27th Div.

Instructions regarding War Diaries and Intelligence Summaries are contained in F. S. Regs., Part II. and the Staff Manual respectively. Title pages will be prepared in manuscript.

Place	Date	Hour	Summary of Events and Information	Remarks and references to Appendices
Bordeaux France	1915 Dec —		Sanitary Section of the Div. entrained for Marseilles to await embarkation.	A.F.
"	7 Dec.		A.D.M.S. D.A.D.M.S. + Office entrain with HeadQuarters 27th Div. for Marseilles to await embarkation.	A.F.
"	9 "		Arrived Marseilles — encamped at Parc Borelly. From this on we are more or less out of communication with units of the Div. Some have sailed, daily some are embarking + en route. They spend a few days in camp at MARSEILLES.	A.F.
"	29 "		Lieut Browne (E. J. BROWNE) admitted to Hospital influenza.	A.F.
"	31st		Colonel (Brevet) F. SMITH D.S.O. army) 9 a.m. from command of us + General Hosp. on Personter + S.M.O. Paris District as A.D.M.S. vice BROWNE. 22/1/16 Lieut Smith ...	A.F.

2353 Wt. W2544/1454 700,000 5/15 D, D, & L. A.D.S.S./Form/C. 2118.

www.ingramcontent.com/pod-product-compliance
Lightning Source LLC
Chambersburg PA
CBHW080854230426
43662CB00013B/2097